ALEXEJ JAWLENSKY
VARIATIONS

CONTENTS

ALEXEJ
JAWLENSKY
VARIATIONS

LOUISIANA MUSEUM
OF MODERN ART

FOREWORD

The story of Alexej Jawlensky (1864-1941) is one that we in a way know so well: that of new painting in the early 20th century. Jawlensky was part of the conversation and, in his own unique way, contributed to painting's revitalization. He was close friends with Wassily Kandinsky and Gabriele Münter, met Matisse, and admired Van Gogh and Munch. He lived in Munich, travelled several times to Paris, and participated in a number of landmark exhibitions, not least the *Erster Deutscher Herbstsalon* in Berlin in 1913. His partner was the painter Marianne Werefkin, and Paul Klee was his lifelong friend. Supposedly, Walter Gropius personally invited him to teach at the Bauhaus. If there was such a thing as modernism bingo, Jawlensky would have a full house.

So why should we revisit an era that has apparently been so thoroughly illuminated? Recent years at the Louisiana have been devoted to artists such as Sonia Delaunay, Gabriele Münter and Marsden Hartley, who all moved in more or less the same circles. These three even participated in the aforementioned *Herbstsalon* in Berlin alongside Jawlensky. From a classical art-historical perspective, you might say that while Kandinsky, Matisse and Van Gogh are the protagonists, Delaunay, Münter, Hartley and Jawlensky are the supporting cast, or at least less celebrated figures.

At the Louisiana, we insist on the complexity of history and art history and the importance of continuing to revisit the stories we think we know so well in order to extract new perspectives. This has been the Louisiana's undertaking for many years, including our exhibitions on Hilma af Klint, Paula Modersohn-Becker and Chaïm Soutine, as well as several group exhibitions about the period. And we do not do it demonstratively – that is, just for the sake of doing it – but because the quality of the works support it.

Jawlensky at the Louisiana homes in on the last 20 or so years of his artistic career because it is here that his work develops in a unique and deeply personal direction. This is a shift away from the Blaue Reiter era, towards something less known and more difficult to classify art historically speaking. It is the story about how Jawlensky gradually finds his own idiom, his own artistic project, which centres on repetition of certain motifs particularly, which Jawlensky practised from 1914 until he stopped painting in the beginning of 1938. These serial paintings are modest in format, small or even tiny, but they are sensational.

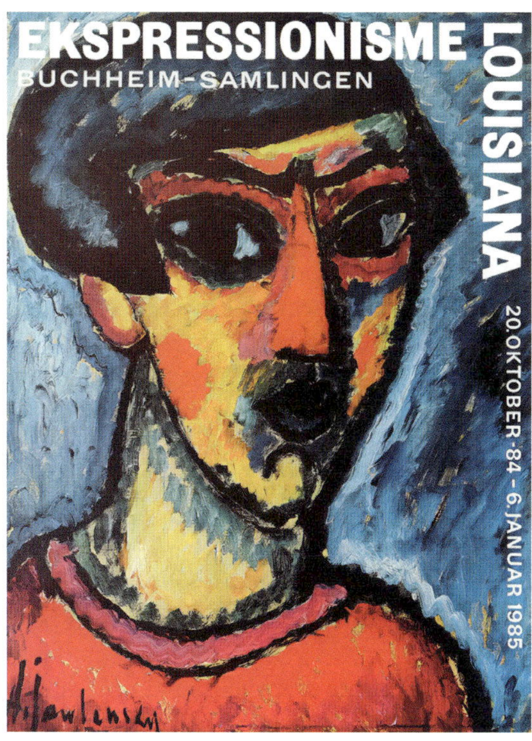

These works have also sparked something in other artists and not only in painters. In 1935, artist-composer John Cage famously (and surprisingly one might add) bought a late work by Jawlensky and wrote a brief letter to him, stating: "I write music. You are my teacher." With Cage's close connection to artists such as Jasper Johns and Mark Rothko it is easy to imagine their conversations about Jawlensky's late *Meditations*. Additionally, light art pioneer James Turrell has confirmed to us that he has been inspired by the Jawlensky works he saw at the Pasadena Art Museum. As Danish painter Alexander Tovborg's contribution to the catalogue demonstrates, Jawlensky continues to play a role for artists even today.

Poul Erik Tøjner, Director, Louisiana Museum of Modern Art
Mathias Ussing Seeberg, Curator, Louisiana Museum of Modern Art

THANKS

This exhibition has been made possible through major and very generous loans from the Im Obersteg Collection at Kunstmuseum Basel and from one of the largest Jawlensky collections in the world at Museum Wiesbaden. The two collections even have very tangible connections to Jawlensky's life. Karl Im Obersteg met Jawlensky in Ascona, Switzerland in 1919 and, particularly through numerous acquisitions, became an important backer for the artist, who struggled financially in the latter part of his life. We are deeply grateful for the support from Stiftung Im Obersteg and Kunstmuseum Basel and our collaboration with Dr Hans Furer and Dr Géraldine Meyer in particular. Jawlensky spent the last 20 years of his life in Wiesbaden, spurred not least by the success of an exhibition there, and here he made his most significant mark on art history. Museum Wiesbaden has also been a great support and help in bringing this exhibition to life, and we especially thank Professor Roman Zieglgänsberger for his guidance. In addition to the robust representation of Jawlensky's works in museums, the painter is also strongly represented in private collections around the world. We thank all the private lenders for supporting our project with their treasured possessions; special thanks to Dr Heinrich A. Vischer for lending eight outstanding works for the exhibition.

For this catalogue Joe Graham wrote an exceptional text on the history of repetition in art, for which we are extremely grateful. The artist Alexander Tovborg also contributed a text about Jawlensky and Byzantine iconography. We are very grateful for this contribution as well.

Finally, we would like to extend our gratitude to the C.L. David Foundation and Collection and to Beckett-Fonden for providing vital support for this exhibition at the Louisiana.

LENDERS

Museum Wiesbaden
Stiftung Im Obersteg, Depositum im Kunstmuseum Basel 2004
Kunstmuseum Basel
Städtische Galerie im Lenbachhaus und Kunstbau München
Kunsthalle Mannheim
Galerie Ludorff, Düsseldorf
Galerie von Vertes, Zürich

Lenders who have wished to remain anonymous

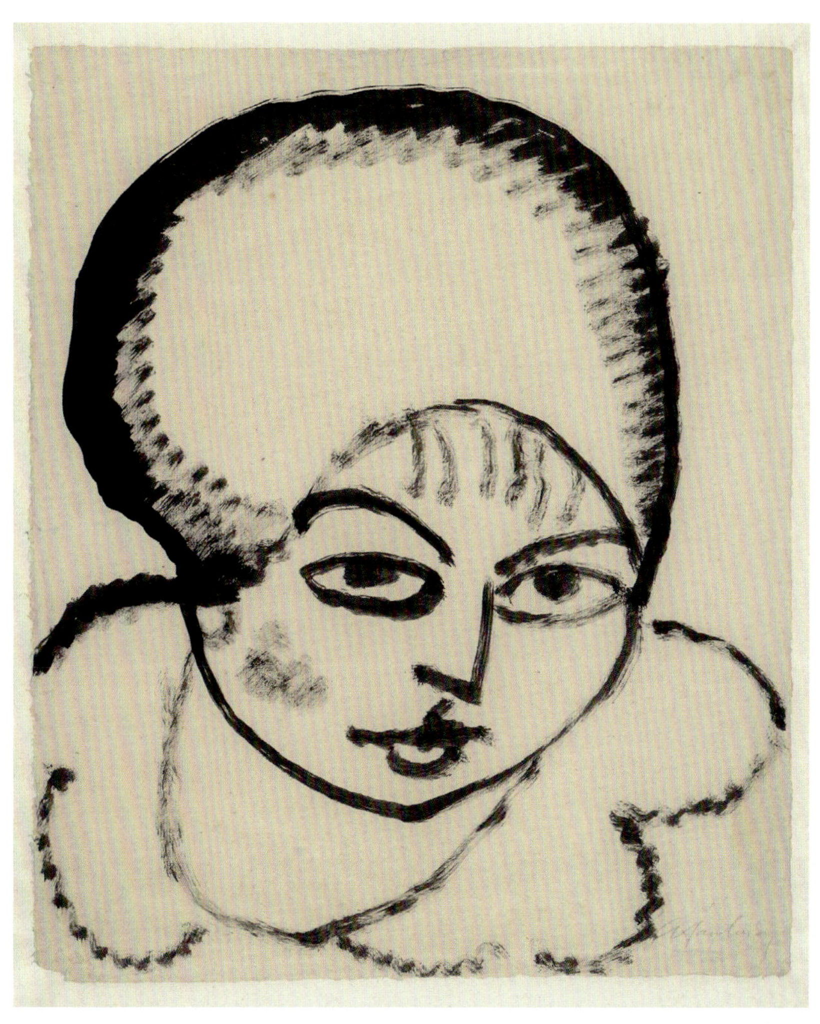

KONSTANTINOWKA WITH HEAD TILTED, C. 1912

STILL LIFE WITH GREEN VASE, C. 1911

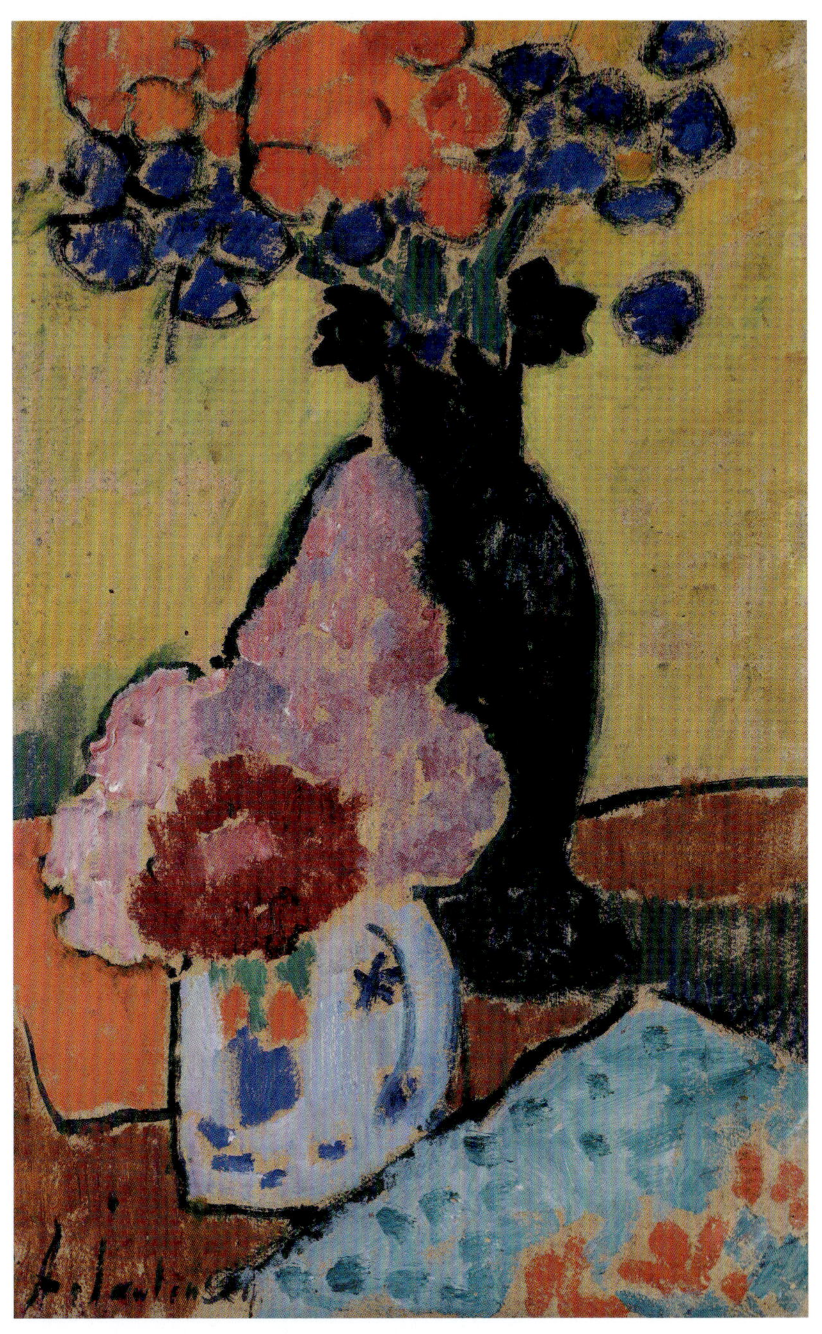

STILL LIFE WITH BLACK VASE, 1909

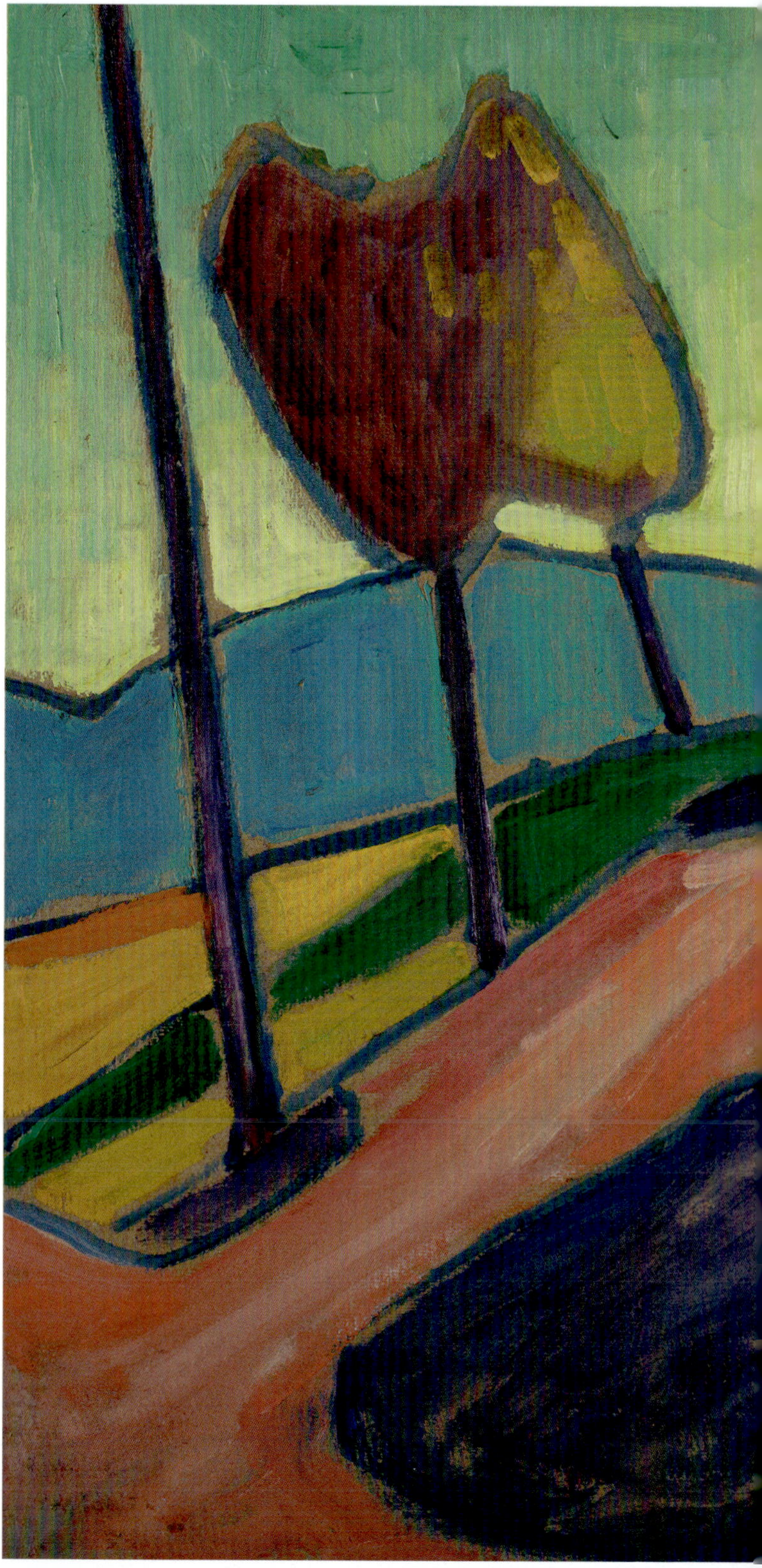

MURNAU LANDSCAPE, 1909

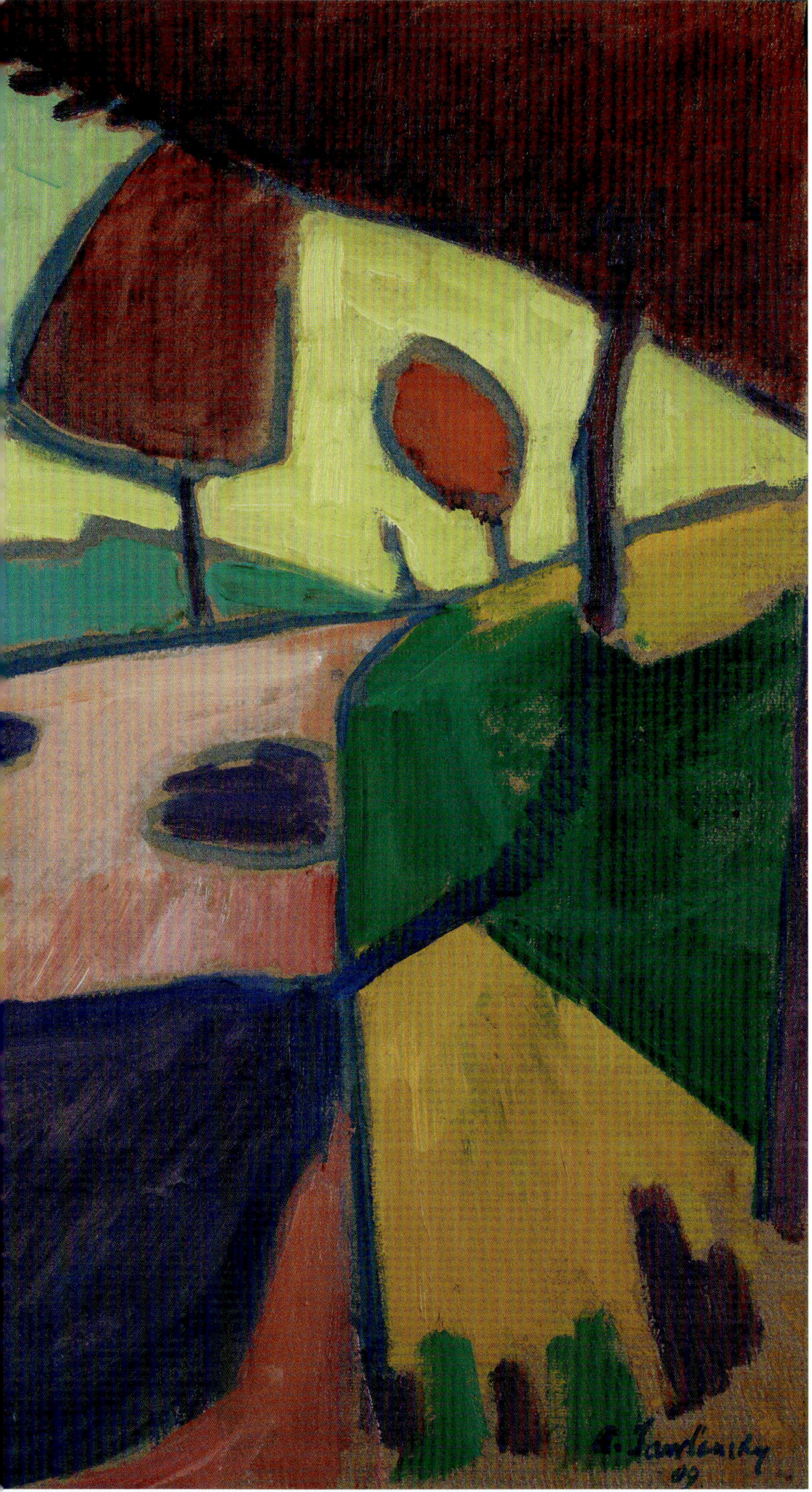

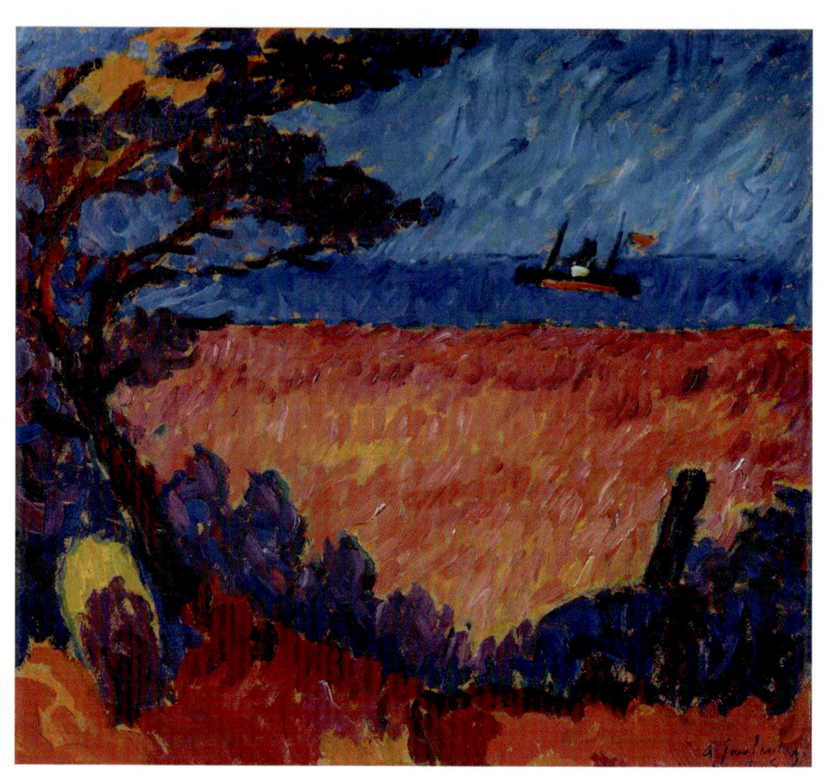

BY THE BALTIC SEA, 1911

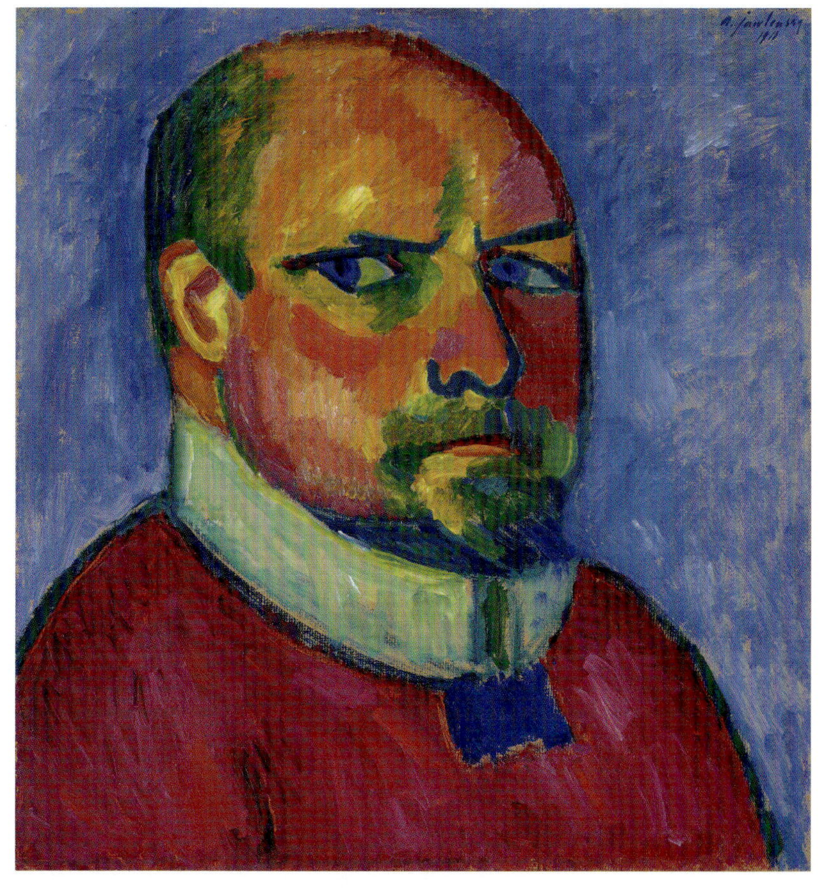

SELF-PORTRAIT, 1911

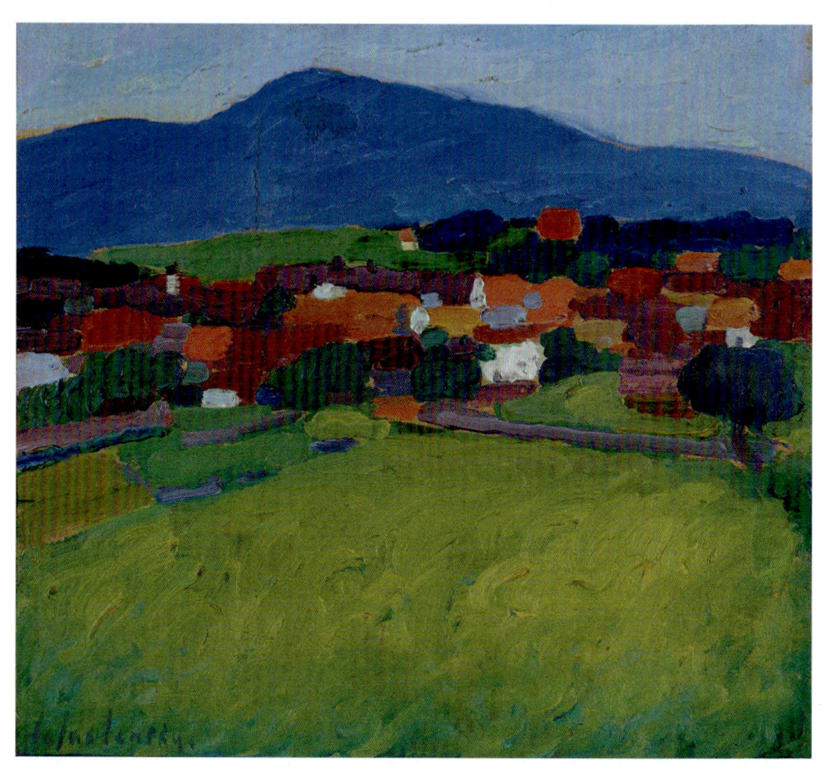

MURNAU VILLAGE, 1908

A VARIATION OF JAWLENSKY: LOOKING AT THE ARTIST

BY MATHIAS USSING SEEBERG

There are many ways to tell the story of an artist's life and work. If the artist had a fairly long life, like Jawlensky, there is a large body of work to look back on and many phases of life to study. In catalogues and exhibitions, this Russian-German artist has been variously Alexej Georgewitsch Jawlensky, Alexej von Jawlensky, Alexei Jawlensky, Alekséy Geórgiyevich Yavlénskiy or Alexej Jawlensky – Алексéй Геóргиевич Явлéнский translated into different languages, with or without the "von" indicating his noble Russian ancestry.

Jawlensky was clearly used to spelling his name, and seeing it spelled, in many different ways. At the groundbreaking 1905 Salon d'Automne in Paris, which marked the breakthrough of the so-called Fauves, he was just Jawlensky, with no first name. At the next year's Salon d'Automne, in the curated section *L'art russe,* he was listed as Alexis Yavlensky. Surely, Jawlensky must have given some thought to how he wanted his name translated, what kind of artist he wanted to be.

The Louisiana's exhibition focusses mainly on the artist's late work, from age 50 until he was no longer able to paint. The last four or so years of his productive life, from age 70 to 74, make up a third of the works shown. The exhibition resists the general art-historical obsession with youth that attributes novelty and revolution to God-given natural talent. Jawlensky did not have an easy beginning. Looking at his complete body of work, you might find yourself agreeing with the classic Miles Davis line, "Man, sometimes it takes you a long time to sound like yourself."[1]

A LONG BEGINNING

Like many other artists, Jawlensky's early career was marked by rapid shifts in painting style. Looking for a style of their own, artists imitated and tried to match others. But Jawlensky was older than most searching artists. At the 1905 Salon d'Automne, he exhibited, among other works, a painting with a striking English title in an otherwise French catalogue. *Mixed Pickles* (1904), measuring a modest 40 × 35 cm, was a still life obviously inspired by Van Gogh. Jawlensky was trying his hand at a rather schematic combination of brushstrokes going in different directions: vertical on the background wall, hori-

1: Quoted in Maria Antónia Lima and Mia Funk (eds.), *Jazz and Literature: An Introduction,* New York: Routledge, 2024, p. 118.

zontal on the tabletop and mainly diagonal on the cup, saucer and bottle, while a plate at the back of the composition is executed in distinct curved strokes. He was 40 years old when he painted this picture, and he still did not know who he was or who he should be. He signed the painting "A. Jawlensky".

The Salon d'Automne was not about him. While his paintings aligned with a new direction in art and were certainly ambitious, the style was clearly not his own. All the same, the Salon was a seminal event, not just for Jawlensky but for modern art in general. The Fauves, including Matisse, Derain and Van Dongen, blew up the notion of what art was and should be, applying wild colours and brushwork to otherwise conventional subjects like landscapes, portraits and still lifes. Matisse was just five years younger than Jawlensky, but many of the other Fauves were much younger. If you think seeing vastly superior work by artists so young would compel Jawlensky to abandon his pursuit, think again.

Instead, he absorbed the lessons of Paris and Fauvism, developing a characteristic Expressionist style over the next few years in prodigious exchange with his peers in Germany. In Dresden, there were the artists of Die Brücke, among them Ernst Ludwig Kirchner, Emil Nolde and Karl Schmidt-Rottluff. In his adopted hometown of Munich, there were the artists in and around Der Blaue Reiter, notably Gabriele Münter, Wassily Kandinsky and Jawlensky's partner, Marianne Werefkin. All these artists produced a wealth of landscapes, still lifes, portraits and large figure paintings. Rejecting realism, they pursued a distinctive style that used colours to convey emotional qualities tied to internal experiences of the world.

The Louisiana's exhibition takes its beginning in those years just before the outbreak of World War I. The earliest work in the exhibition, *Dorf Murnau*, was painted in 1908 in Murnau am Staffelsee, where Jawlensky and Werefkin spent three consecutive summers with Münter and Kandinsky. The first chapter revolves around Jawlensky's participation in the Southern German avant-garde, presenting landscapes, still lifes and portraits painted in exemplary varieties of Expressionism. There are many terrific works from this period. Historically, they have been Jawlensky's most frequently exhibited works and have commanded the highest prices at auction.

These works are typically included in the narrative about the new pictorial language developed in Munich. While Jawlensky contributed to this development, he is not considered one of its main architects. We can identify his style and recognise his talent, but he is still only one among many others. Accordingly, the exhibition's first chapter is also its shortest. It marks a real beginning, if only the germ of what was to come.

ALEXEJ JAWLENSKY
MIXED PICKLES, 1904
OIL ON CANVAS, 40.1 × 35.1 CM
PRIVATE COLLECTION

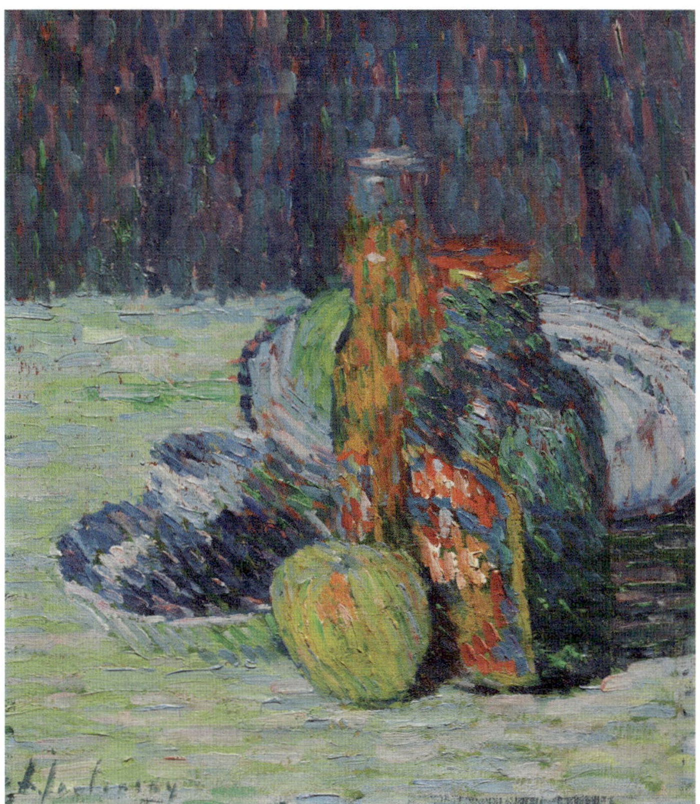

A NEW ARTIST

At the outbreak of World War I in August 1914, Jawlensky and Werefkin fled to Switzerland. In the small town of Saint-Prex on Lake Geneva, Jawlensky, now 50, realised that he could no longer paint in his accustomed manner and made a clean break with his previous work. The second part of the exhibition looks at a whole new artist.

In his memoirs, Jawlensky describes the "suffering" he had undergone[2] as one reason for his change of tack. Perhaps it was also a liberation from the ambitions of the avant-garde. There was no Kandinsky or Franz Marc to measure up to now, no artists' groups to bicker with. Jawlensky had to find his own path. Remarkably, rather than making large-scale, stand-alone paintings, he devoted the rest of his life almost exclusively to painting serial images on a very modest scale and often on paper. While financial considerations may have influenced his use of paper instead of canvas, and without ascribing undue conceptual intention to this choice, I would like to mention the American artist Nancy Spero, who rejected canvas for paper because of the connotations of canvas to heroic, masculine painting. Intentionally or not, Jawlensky's work has a similar effect: there was a different intent with the painting, even before paint was applied.

Jawlensky's first try at an entirely new kind of painting was a series of landscapes in unusual, small, vertical formats. Over and over again, he painted the view from his house in Saint-Prex. In the first works, the connection between the painting and the view remained intact. These are pictures of what is seen, experienced. There is a road, trees, a gate. There is up and down, near and far. In a way, Jawlensky is like Monet in Rouen painting the changing light on the cathedral from the window of his room, again and again.

Jawlensky called this project *Variations*. Over time, the pictures lost their close connection to what was seen. He stopped looking out the window entirely. The remaining link between the pictures and their starting point, the view, is apparent only when comparing later and earlier versions. Jawlensky had not only embarked on a series of works of the same image; he had created an actual serial artwork, in which the real pleasure lies exactly in comparing multiple versions. By choosing paper as a support, and through repetition, Jawlensky also moved away from grand, heavy art history and the notion of the singular "masterpiece" that defines it. The individual work exists as part of a greater whole. Titling his works, Jawlensky made it clear

2: Clemens Weiler, *Jawlensky: Heads, Faces, Meditations*,
Karlsruhe: Pall Mall Press, 1971, p. 101.

that they are not meant to stand alone. *Variations* implies a musicality of painting with repetition and constant change. The composer Arnold Schönberg was close with the artists of Munich. In music, he wrote, repetition combined with variation "shows that different things can arise from one thing [aus Einem Verschiedenes], through its development, through the musical vicissitudes it undergoes, through generating new figures".[3]

The *Variations* – he painted more than 300 – was Jawlensky's first truly original artwork. Repetition became the artistic device he would use for the rest of his life as a painter, while the subject to be repeated had yet to be determined.

THE FACE TAKES FORM

Portraits are prominent in Jawlensky's work. He is best known for the portraits in the years before World War I. However, abandoning his usual method after arriving in Switzerland also put an end to the colourful portraits, almost overnight. Even so, he did not completely set aside his former interest. After he and Werefkin moved to Zurich in 1917, Jawlensky began experimenting with serial portraits, alongside his *Variations*. *Mystical Heads*, he called them, stylised portraits of women he knew. As several art historians have noted, the heads in this series can still be imagined as attached to bodies. They have little of the conceptual rigidity of the *Variations* and can mainly be regarded as a step on the road. Because he was not done with the face. Late in life Jawlensky famously wrote, "great art can only be painted with religious feeling. And that I could only bring to the human face".[4] He knew what he wanted to do, but not how to do it yet.

The spiritual feeling that Jawlensky sought to evoke in his work compelled him to separate the head from the body and fully sever the connection to portraiture. The face could not belong to a specific person. In his next series of works, *Saviour's Face*, Jawlensky depicted the face exclusively from the front, cropped at the forehead and chin. As was likely intended, these faces tend to have an ambiguous, androgynous quality. The spiritual or divine face exists beyond any conception of gender. The face is not just a face but "the whole universe. In the face the whole universe becomes manifest".[5]

Saviour's Face presents Jawlensky's first truly serial faces, though their form was still not as tight as in the *Variations*. He varied elements in the new series, such as whether to include hair or a crown of thorns on the forehead. But the most significant change he made, and

3: Áine Heneghan, "Rethinking Repetition: Interrogating Schoenberg's Writings", *Perspectives of New Music* 57, no. 1, 2019, p. 27. 4: Clemens Weiler, p. 108. 5: Ibid., p. 56.

the most crucial to his future work, was to begin painting faces with closed eyes. Soon, Jawlensky was exclusively painting closed-eyed faces. This led to an even more stylised image in his second-to-last major series, *Abstract Heads*. Once the series was firmly established, Jawlensky stopped painting his *Variations* altogether. He had found a project to replace them.

ICONS

Occupying Jawlensky from the early 1920s to 1933, *Abstract Heads* recall Bauhaus and the African masks that fascinated so many artists at the time. The paintings were carefully designed, with meticulously applied colour combinations on a fixed geometry. As a result, each picture is both recognisable and entirely new.

The series' title, a curious oxymoron, may pay lip service to abstraction, but Jawlensky had no desire to achieve actual abstraction like his fellow Russian Kandinsky. For the remainder of his life, Jawlensky maintained a link to figuration, even if it became less clear in his final years. In his memoirs, he stated that he was "Russian born. As such my heart and soul was always close to old Russian art, to Russian icons [...] It was this art that gave me my tradition". The Christian icons provide the foundation for Jawlensky's effort to create spiritual images of similar power. As the Finnish art historian Sixten Ringbom notes, there is "little in official Christian religion as such to inspire or justify a non-objective mode of expression. The Christian artist is more likely to conceive his subject in figurative terms. Implicit in the Christian conception of art is the principle that what can be represented at all, can be represented figuratively, that is, as a narrative or symbolical image."[6] Jawlensky's upbringing, his tradition and his aim kept figuration in the picture.

Abstract Heads and his later *Meditations* have many allusions to Christianity, but they also reference other cultures and religions, suggesting that Jawlensky was less orthodox than his background might imply. Like so many others at the time, he was, in general, theosophically inclined. Jawlensky famously practiced a form of meditative yoga,[7] and his interest in Christian icons likely stemmed more from their communicative power, their ability to point to the invisible, to the spiritual, than their Christian message per se.

6: Sixten Ringbom, *The Sounding Cosmos: A Study in the Spiritualism of Kandinsky and the Genesis of Abstract Painting*, Stockholm: Bokförlaget Stolpe, 2022, p. 22. 7: Jill Lloyd, "Jawlensky's Late Work: Painting in Series", in: Vivian Endicott Barnett (ed.), *Alexei Jawlensky*, Munich: Prestel Verlag, 2017, p. 53.

LAST WORKS

Clearly, the *Abstract Heads* were painstakingly created. While the form was largely given from one work to the next, Jawlensky explored a wide variety of colour combinations with very refined, carefully applied brushstrokes. However, this process was brought to an end by his debilitating arthritis. *Abstract Heads* had to be replaced by something new, something simpler, the essential. Jawlensky had no doubt himself that what he achieved was a triumph and labelled his last paintings "important works". His colleagues felt the same. In 1936, his old friend Kandinsky wrote to him about one of these final works, "I like your little picture very much. The dark and scintillating colours are wonderful. The whole impression is one of great depth and at the same time of a lively freshness. I see with awe and amazement that in spite of your agonizing illness you have retained the strength that keeps soul and mind active. I bow low before the power of your inner spiritual life."[8]

The *Meditations* are by far Jawlensky's most extensive serial work. He made more than 1,000 of these paintings. The third and final chapter of the exhibition focusses on them. The refined face of *Abstract Heads* was reduced to a rough sketch of a face, executed in broad black brushstrokes resembling a cross, the spaces between them filled with different combinations of colour. That these works can even be identified as "heads" is in large part because we know what they evolved from. Indeed, they are much more abstract than the ones in the *Abstract Heads* series. Underscoring their connection to religious icons, Jawlensky even painted a few *Meditations* on gold leaf.

In its subject matter and repetition, this project is linked to religious liturgy, which involves performing the same ritual actions over and over again. Jawlensky even described these pictures as "prayer in colour". Before painting, he meditated to put himself into a religious state of mind. Hence, aside from their powerful visual qualities, the paintings are also traces of something that has taken place. Yves Klein, who also modelled his works on icons, described his paintings as the ashes of his art. Likewise, Jawlensky's *Meditations* can be seen as the remains of a spiritual ritual, a performative painting practice centred on painful repetition, even a form of flagellation, which brings to mind the obsessively repetitive work of Roman Opalka. In describing the process himself, Jawlensky wrote, "God knows how long I shall be able to hold a brush. I work with ecstasy and with tears in my eyes and I go on until darkness falls and envelops me."[9]

8: Clemens Weiler, p. 111. 9: Ibid., p. 82.

The *Meditations* are small, some even tiny. Jawlensky painted them for just four years, from 1934 until he was no longer able to paint in early 1938, yet they constitute a third of the works in this exhibition. Despite their modest size, they can rightly be called "action paintings", in deliberate reference to postwar American painters. Jawlensky's (impaired) body is palpably present in these works, much like Jackson Pollock's body is present in his, evidence of his dancing around, spattering paint on the canvas. Jawlensky even called one of his *Meditations*, *In Memory of My Ailing Hands (N. 5)* (1934), to make an apparent link between body and work, beyond the obvious observation that all works are created by bodies.

So much can be derived from the works in this exhibition, not least the simple pleasure of looking at the different series of images. Through the process of looking, as Jawlensky has staged it, we recognize the fundamental importance of moving between the variations, of comparing one to the other. The distinction between sameness and difference, a key issue in painting, is in the eye of the beholder.

Through our focus, a particular artist emerges – a variation of Jawlensky, one among many. Having purchased a *Meditation* in 1935, the artist-composer (and Schönberg student) John Cage wrote to Jawlensky in broken German, "I can't write German or speak it, but I'm overjoyed because I've bought one of your pictures: Now it is in me. I write music. You are my teacher." Cage addressed the letter to "Herr Jawlinski".

Mathias Ussing Seeberg is Curator and Head of Research at the Louisiana Museum of Modern Art. In addition to the Alexej Jawlensky exhibition, he has curated exhibitions with artists including Marsden Hartley, J.A. Jerichau, Arthur Jafa, Alex Da Corte and Firelei Báez.

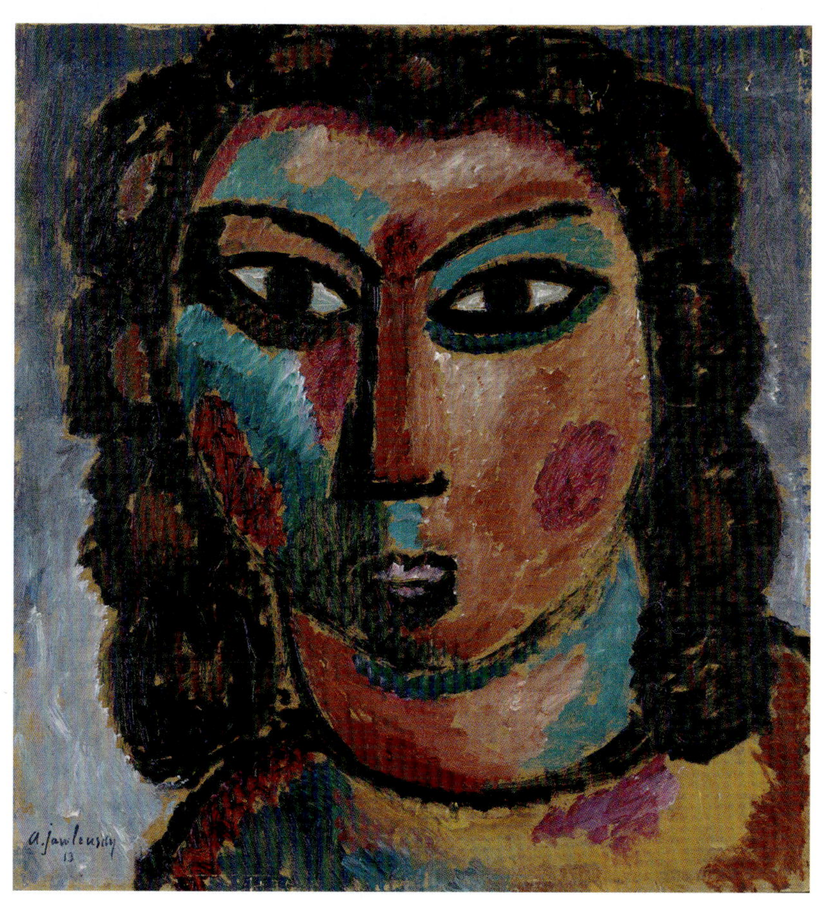

BROWN LOCKS, 1913

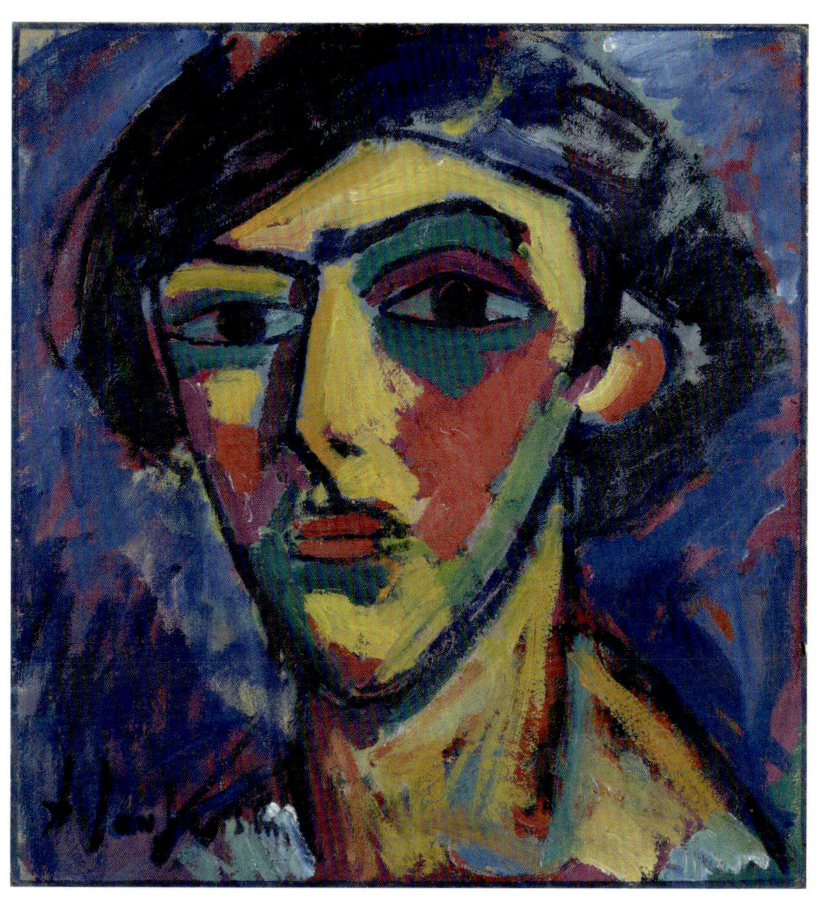

HEAD OF A YOUTH, 1911

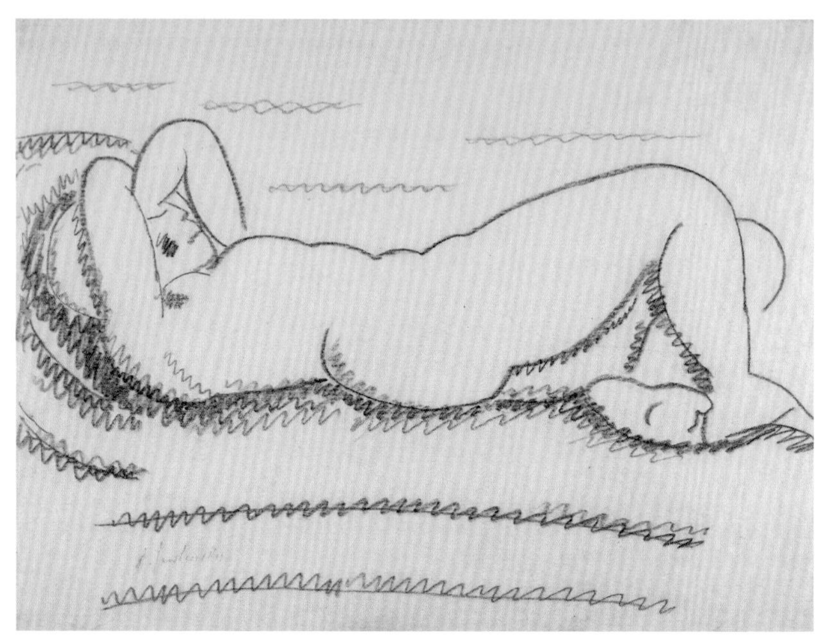

RECLINING, C. 1912

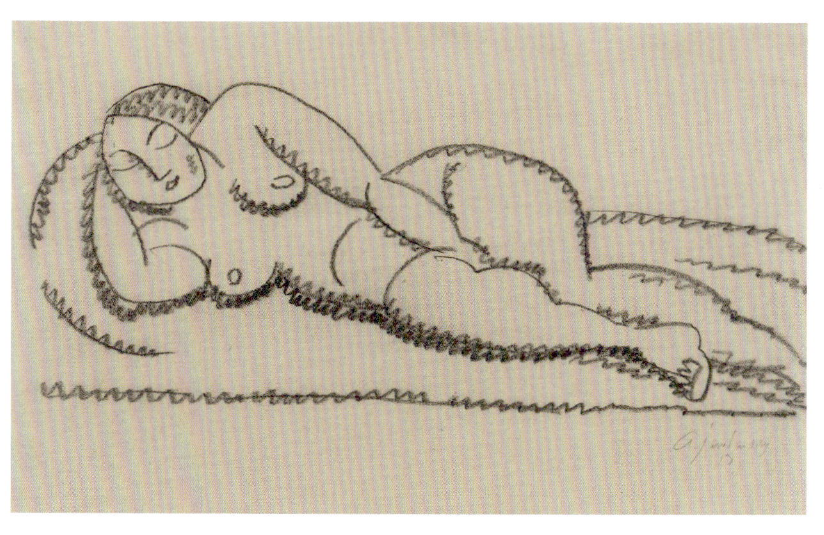

RECLINING FEMALE NUDE, 1913

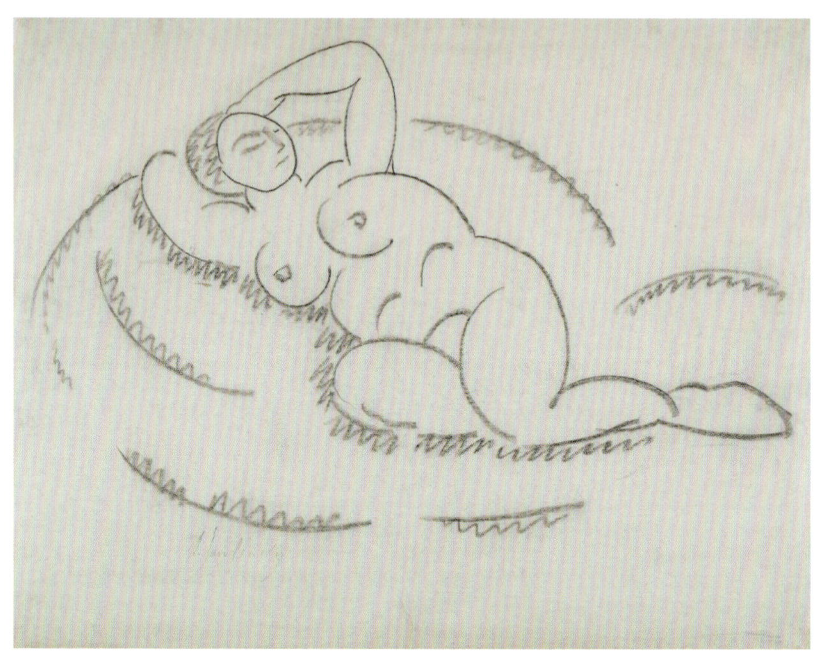

RECLINING FEMALE NUDE WITH ARMS ABOVE HEAD, C. 1912

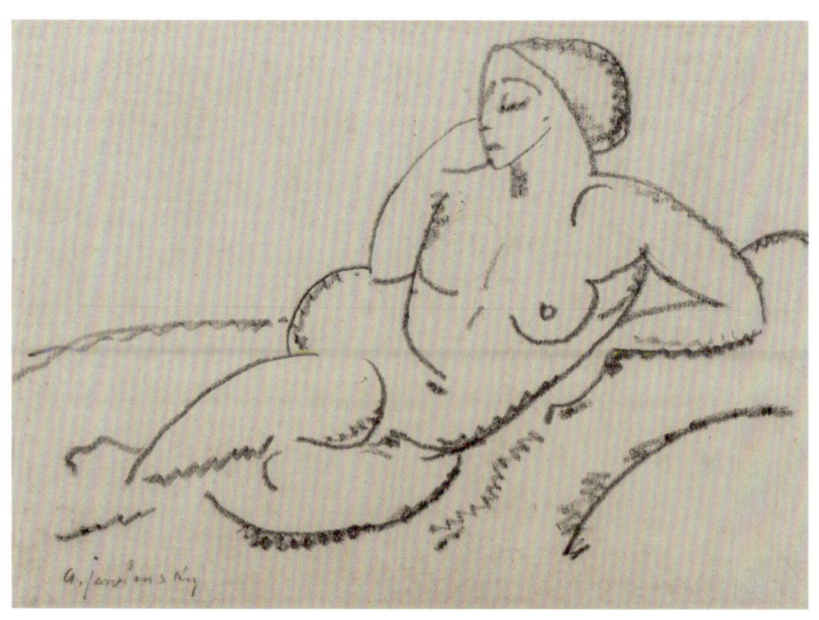

RECLINING FEMALE NUDE, C. 1913

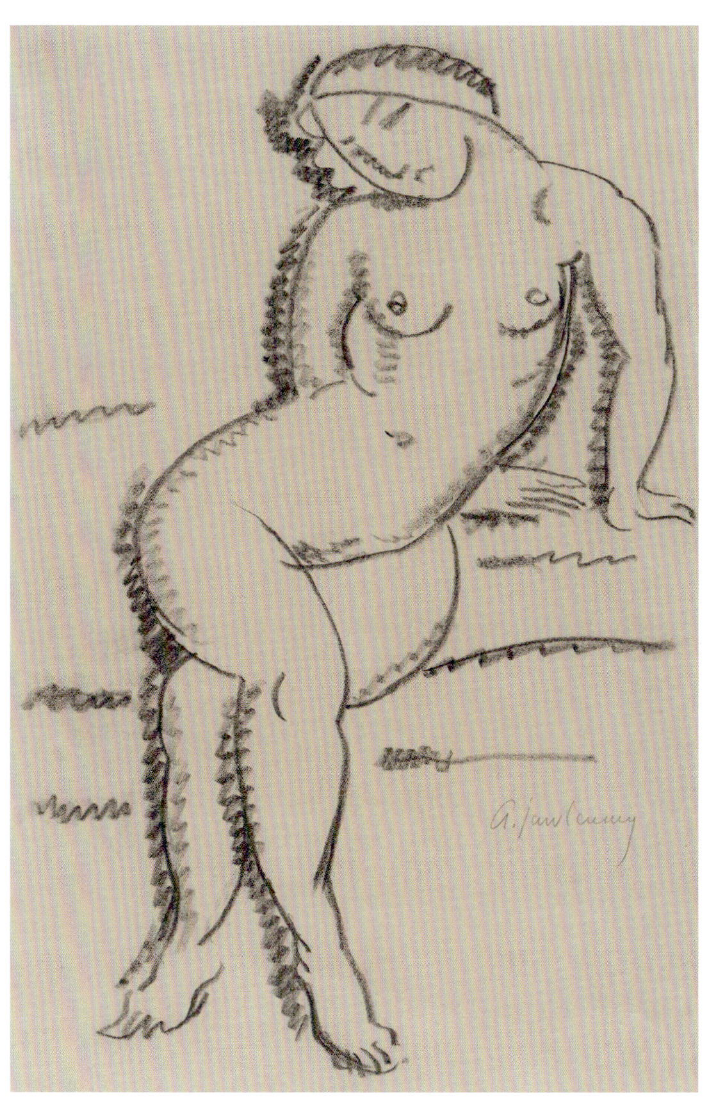

SITTING FEMALE NUDE, 1913

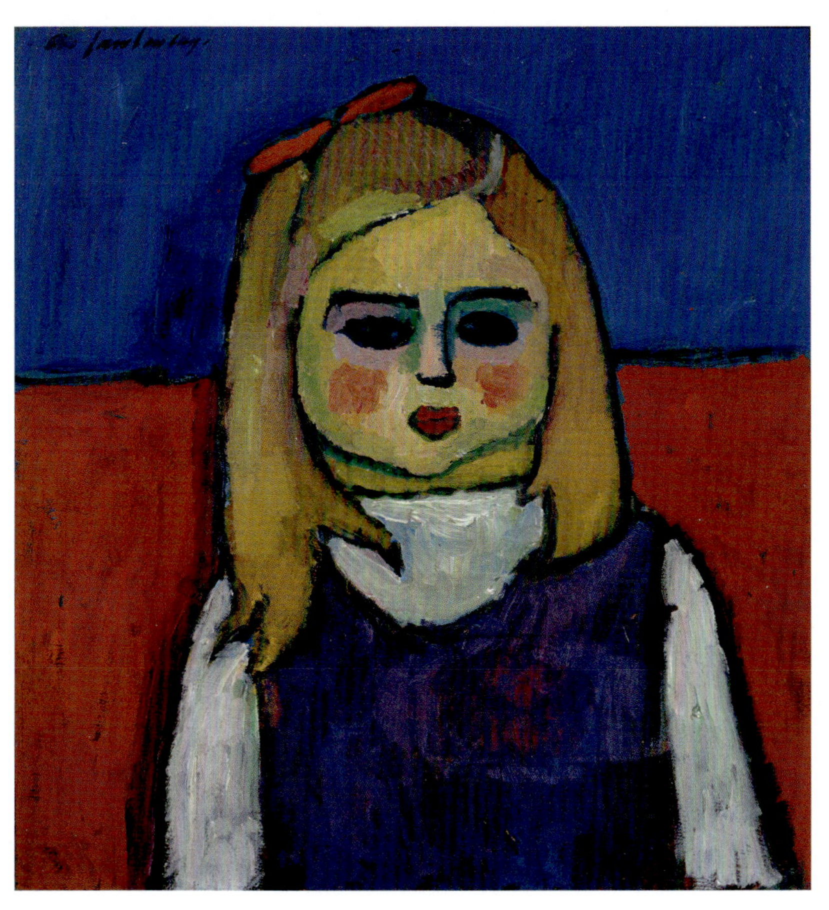

CHILD, C. 1909

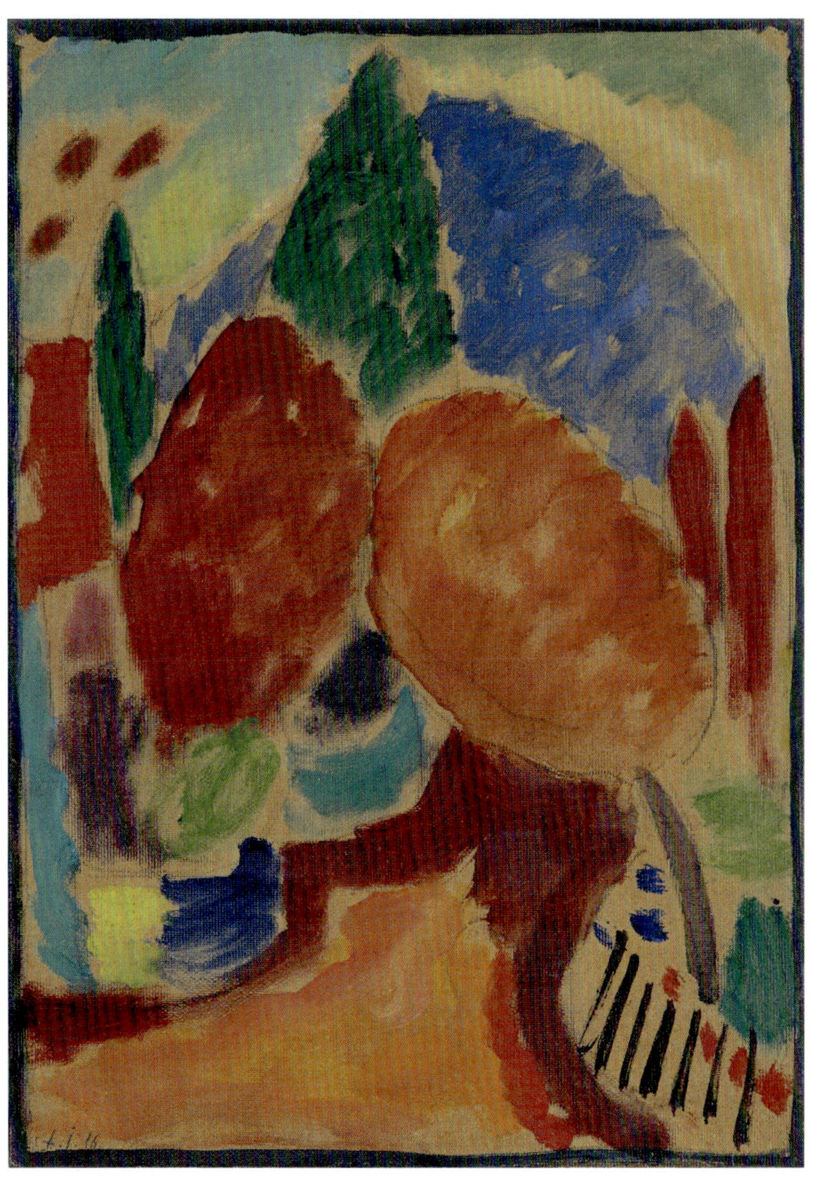

VARIATION: THE ORANGE ROAD, 1916

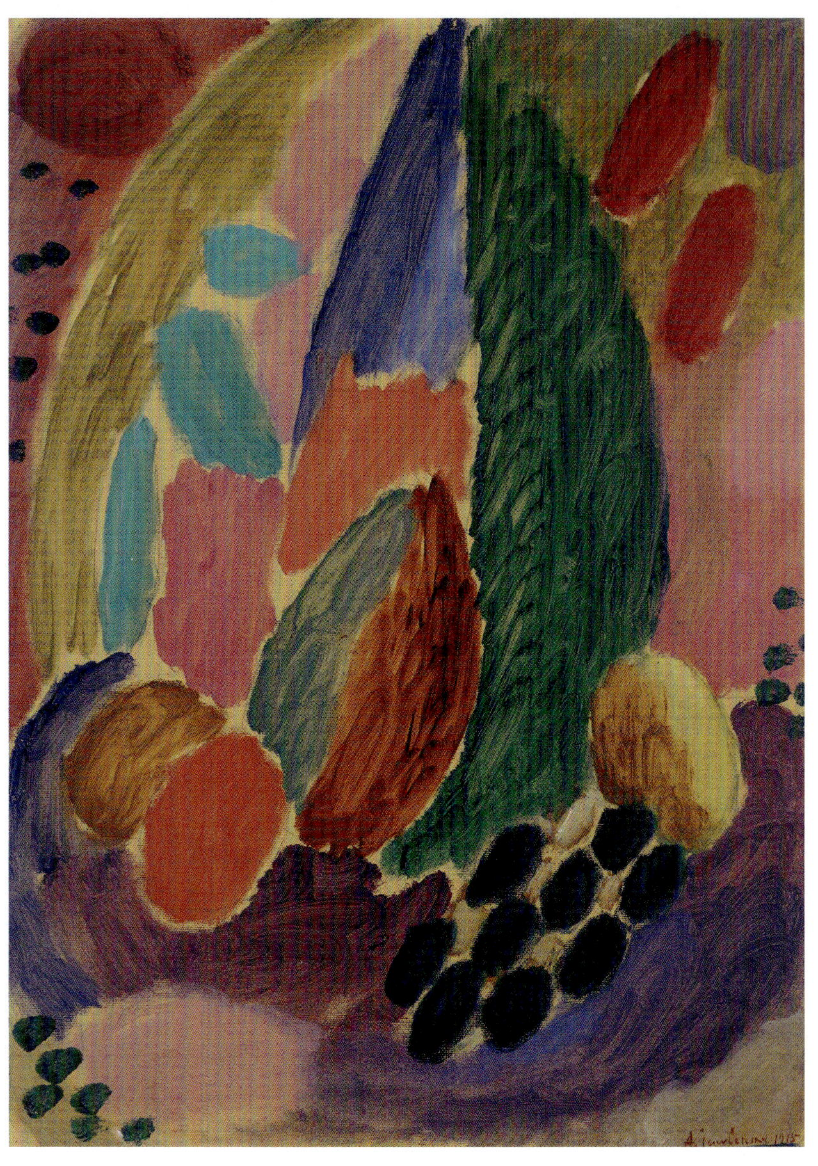

LARGE VARIATION, 1915

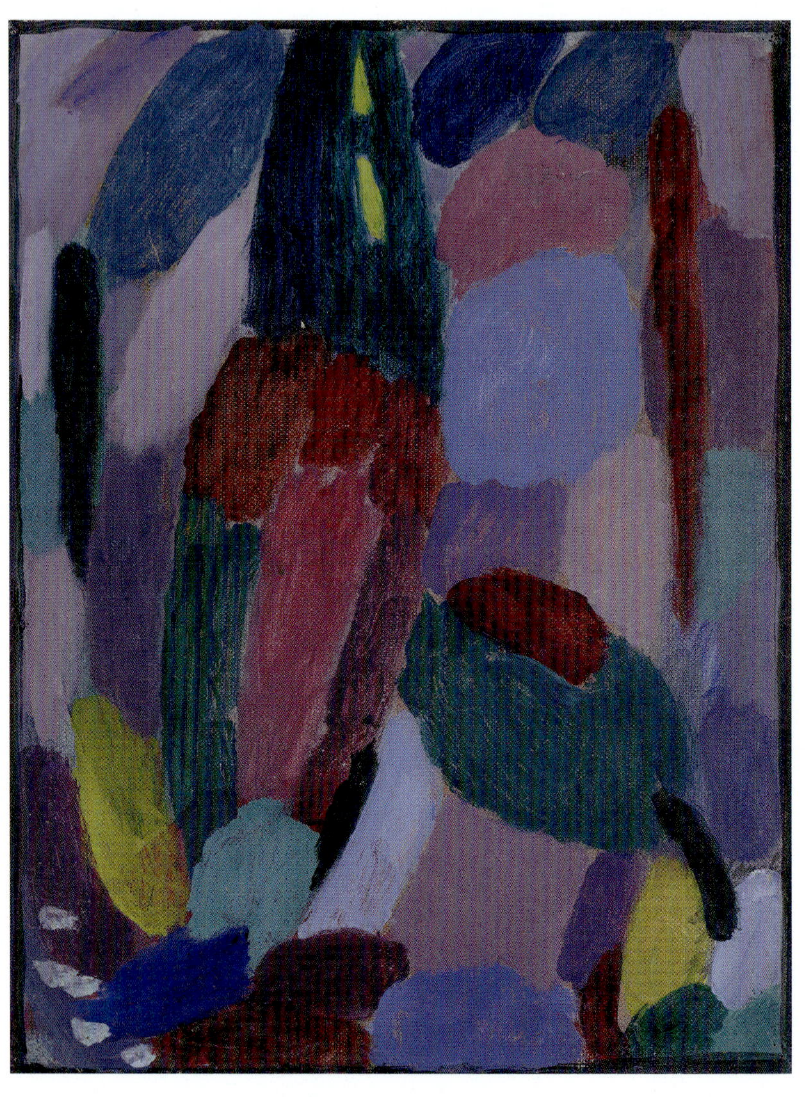

VARIATION: TWILIGHT, C. 1916

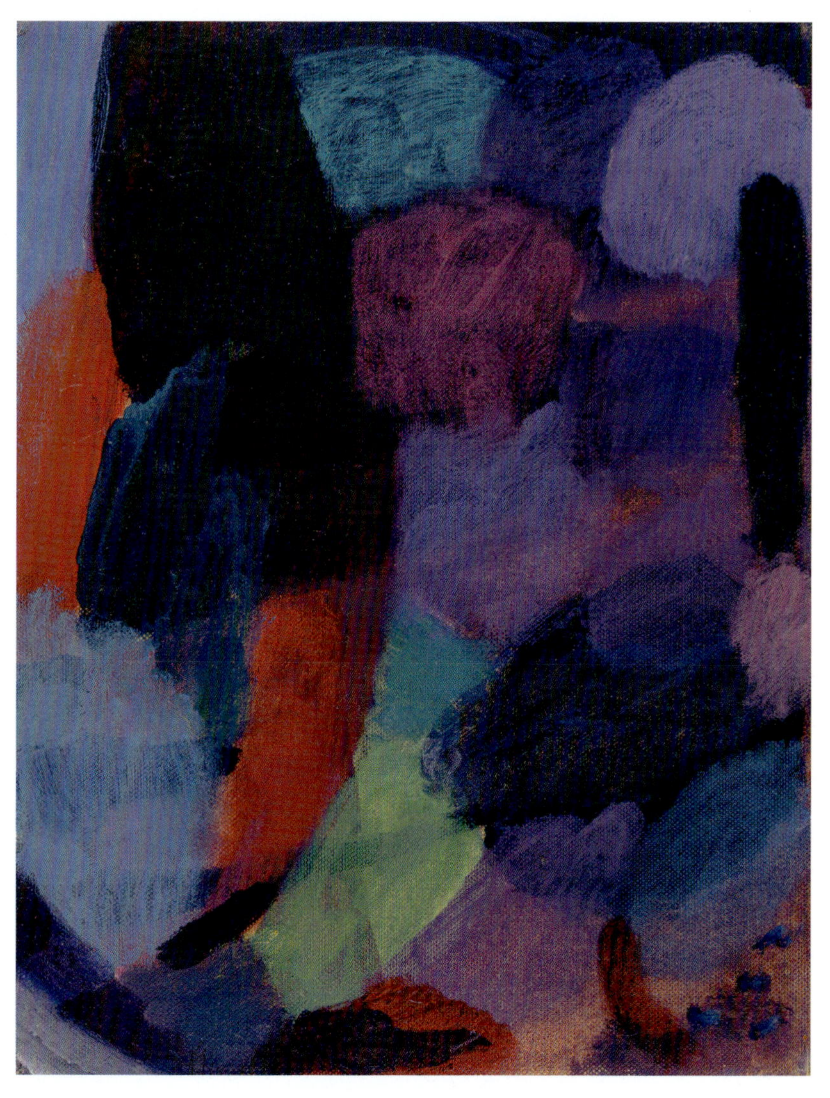

VARIATION: NIGHT, 1916

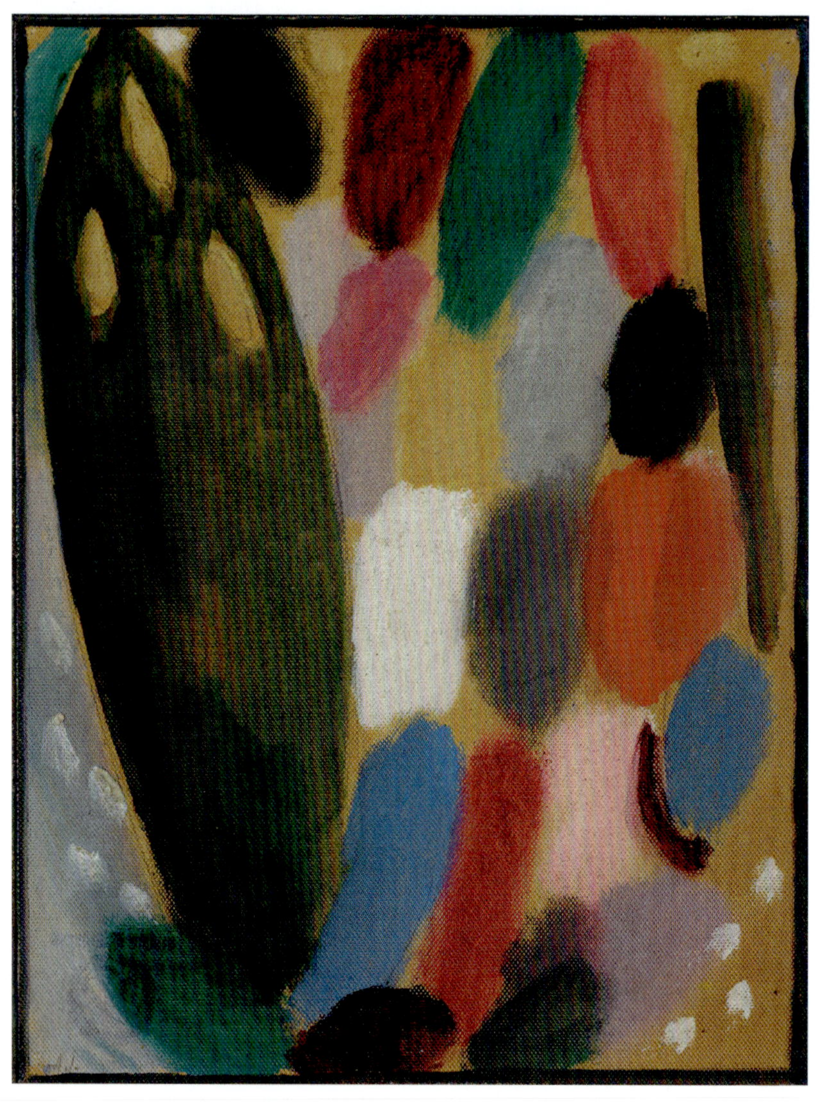

VARIATION: PURPLE-GOLD (AUTUMN), C. 1918

THE SERIAL LEGACY OF ALEXEJ JAWLENSKY

BY JOE GRAHAM

Without needing to be nominated as the first Western artist to develop the idea of *serial art*, the paintings produced by Claude Monet at the close of the 19th century certainly paved the way for our contemporary understanding of this beguiling artistic phenomenon. Beginning with Monet rather than Piet Mondrian also allows us to better position Alexej Jawlensky's own vital contribution to the genre which emerged not long after, constituting as it does an arguably greater level of success in this regard. Jawlensky was the first artist to use the highly repetitive image characteristic of later serial image painters like Josef Albers or Andy Warhol, wherein the idea of an expandable order and the formalization of infinite duration takes centre stage. Instead of seeking to confront the concept of seriality per se, Monet was engaged with another concern for which the serial method proved useful: namely, capturing the impression of instantaneity. Characteristic of this aim is the *Haystacks* series, primarily the 25 canvases begun at the end of summer in 1890 in the fields adjacent to Monet's home in Giverny, and continued during the following spring. In capturing the changing impression of light as it gently coloured these iconic forms that lay scattered across the Normandy landscape, Monet sought compositional stability. He needed a framework upon which such a fleeting, ephemeral impression might be presented as a series of instants, leading to his discovery of the series as a tool fit for the task.

Monet's *Haystacks* presents us with a unified subject matter across the series as a whole, but where each individual painting offers us a new iteration of that same subject matter, framed as the subtle shift of light upon a multifaceted surface. This combination of simultaneity and succession constitutes one of the defining criteria for serial art, indicating a work which is spatially extended as a series of discrete units, yet durationally encountered by a beholder as a unified entity.[1] Monet's desire to capture instantaneity in his paintings propelled the development of serial art in a similarly iterative fashion, as each problem related to the workings of a series generated a new type of serial artwork in response. For example, in order to capture instantaneity, Monet decided that too much variation between each successive stage was to be avoided. In this regard the haystacks at Giverny proved difficult, given there were far too many environmental forces

1: Joe Graham, *Serial Drawing: Space, Time and the Art Object*, London: Bloomsbury Visual Arts, 2021.

at play: the movement of shadows cast by each stack, the wind rippling the grass, hay and foliage, the changing colours of the same, etc. In attempting to counter these factors and simplify matters, Monet took up residence in a room above a milliner's shop in the city of Rouen. This afforded him a fine view out of the window onto the facade of Rouen Cathedral, setting the stage for a further iteration of the method he had previously deployed.

The colossal stone walls of the famous cathedral provided Monet with the stability he was seeking – a geometrically ordered facade whose appearance retained a number of all-important organic elements but which was better able to resist the multiple impulses of nature to which the *Haystacks* were prey. The vertical window out of which he gazed stabilized his composition as it played itself out across a suite of canvasses, thus producing the *Rouen Cathedral* series, an icon of French Impressionism and Monet's most exhaustive example of the serial genre. Between 1892 and 1893 approximately 40 paintings of the cathedral were begun in his rented room in Rouen before being reworked later in his studio, with 20 being selected for exhibition at Durand-Ruel, his Paris gallery, in 1895. They all depict the same frontal area of the cathedral facade in layers of encrusted paint, yet they differ from each other quite dramatically when inspected up close, with colour, hue and the angle at which the facade appears all undergoing constant variation. Monet's effort to capture the dynamic, transitory quality of light upon a fixed object resulted in a shimmering, fluxing surface – one that is *seen serially* across the work as a whole when the effects of one canvas are compared against another.

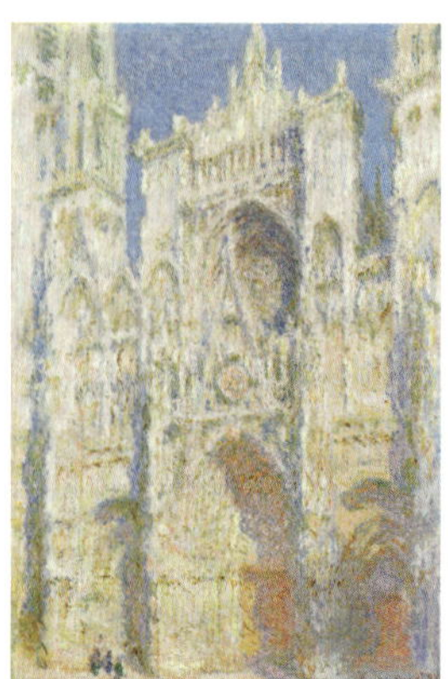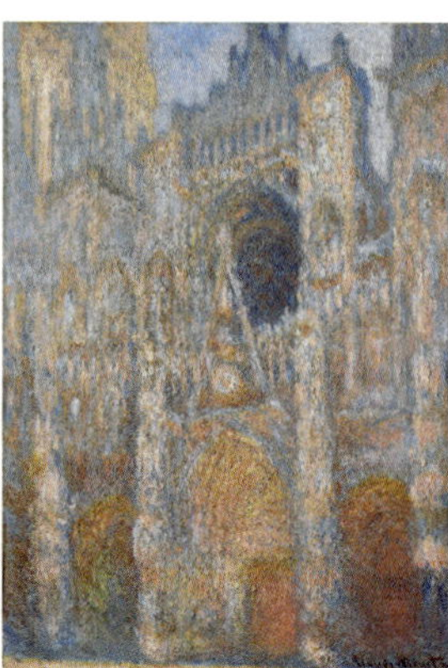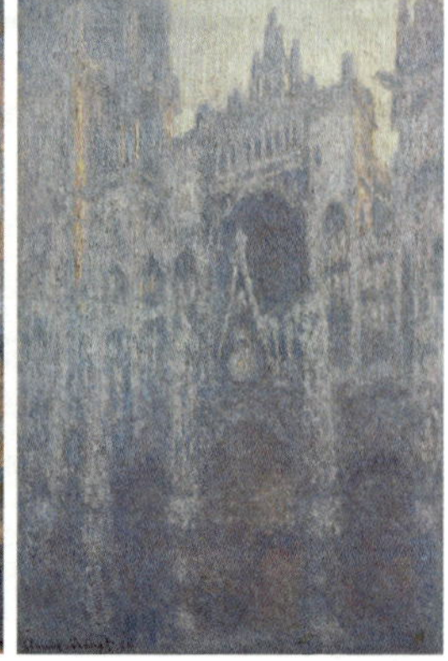

JAWLENSKY'S SERIAL VISION

The precise influence of Monet's series on Jawlensky's own artistic trajectory is hard to pin down without a degree of conjecture. The seemingly obvious differences between their approach as artists – the former being presented as purely "empirical" in attitude while the latter is lauded as being "mystic, romantic" – duly comes up for mention by later commentators.[2] Unlike his *Blue Four* peers Kandinsky and Klee, Jawlensky did not produce any theoretical writings. Nevertheless, he was for a time a student in Paris at Matisse's teaching studio, living there in 1907 before returning again in 1911, while a number of Monet's later works were exhibited in Paris between 1900 and 1912. Of particular interest is the manner in which, after 1914, Jawlensky not only produces work in series, but does so in a manner that consistently deploys a firmly fixed viewpoint using the portrait format, a la the *Rouen Cathedral* series. Although Jawlensky's comparative fame rests largely on his so-called German Expressionist period between 1908 to 1913, when considered in the context of serial art's development during the 20th century, the work he produced from 1914 until around three years before his death in 1941 constitute the highlights of his career. The principal body of this output is three large series of landscapes and heads, known in English as *Variations* (1914-1920), *Abstract Heads* (1916-1933) and a final series, *Meditations* (1934-1937). Prior to 1914 Jawlensky had been producing expressionistic portraits, mostly complete heads of women. The earliest examples date from the decade immediately preceding the turn of the century, whereupon a decided visual emphasis is placed upon the relationship between the frame and the edge of the canvas. But while such structural elements constitute a key theme of Jawlensky's work at the time, what emerged in 1914 was quite unlike anything that had ever come before.

Courtesy of a war-enforced exile in Saint-Prex, Switzerland, Jawlensky moved almost overnight to commence the *Variations*, a series of landscape paintings that pictured the world from a single, fixed viewpoint. While the uniqueness of the human visage was celebrated in the portraits of women Jawlensky painted prior, the *Variations* renounced this and other traits of his German Expressionist period at a stroke. And, while the format of these works appears highly redolent of the serial artwork Monet had completed and exhibited by this point, there was one crucial difference: unlike Monet, Jawlensky's series declined to present the beholder with any clear indication as to the passing of time. Measuring on average 36 cm by 26 cm, each individual *Variation* depicts what appears to be the exact

2: James T. Demetrion, *Alexie Jawlensky: A Centennial Exhibition*, Pasadena: Pasadena Art Museum, 1964, p. 13.

same scene, using the same format and the same restricted colour palette. The scene is the view from Jawlensky's window in Saint-Prex. In place of the head, what Jawlensky offers across the *Variations* is a consistently recognizable configuration of coloured elements, synonymous with trees, bushes and other forms of vegetation. These bob and sway with unceasing regularity from canvas to canvas, albeit without the use of a horizon line, or indeed any form of substantial separation between object and ground.

However, the "world of pure shape" generated by the *Variations* remains far removed from being a mere formal device for selecting and abstracting key elements of the Swiss landscape.[3] On the contrary, what Jawlensky puts forth at this point in his career is a distinctly "serial vision", the first of its kind.[4] In contrast with the earlier portraits of (different) women, where a number of inconsistencies allow us to understand they were painted directly from observation, the *Variations* create a sense of distance between the original scene and the series of individual paintings based upon it, each of which continued to emerge long after Jawlensky had left Saint-Prex, first for Zurich in 1917 and then on to Ascona. Rather than seeking to capture the varying conditions of a landscape as it undergoes change, what Jawlensky renders instead is a set of "simultaneous views".[5] The sense of infinite duration which is shaped by this decision works in tandem with the uncanny sense of distance that the series opens up, producing in turn an intimation of the sublime. Just as patches of bright colour seem to gather towards the lower centre of each *Variation* in memory of the lost horizon line which ought to be found at that location, the beholder searches in vain amongst the parade of bulbous, colourful shapes for any trace of the passing of time. In the words of one of his most important interlocutors, "at the same time that Jawlensky bows to nature's irregularities, he strips her of her ability to change".[6]

FORMALISED SIMILARITY

As the *Variations* were progressing, Jawlensky also submitted his series of heads to a process of quite radical simplification. Gradually they began to lose their idiosyncratic qualities as portraits of individuals, and began to enter a realm of structural simplification and balanced colour that retains much in common with the landscape series whilst simultaneously departing from it. The *Abstract Heads* rendered in diagrammatic form that which Jawlensky had previously sought to express in more traditional terms. The nose becomes a simple line which occurs parallel to the canvas sides. The mouth is transformed into a horizontal line, while hair, eyebrows and eyes all become abstracted to a similar degree, becoming either horizontal or diagonal. With eyes closed, the head in this series becomes akin to

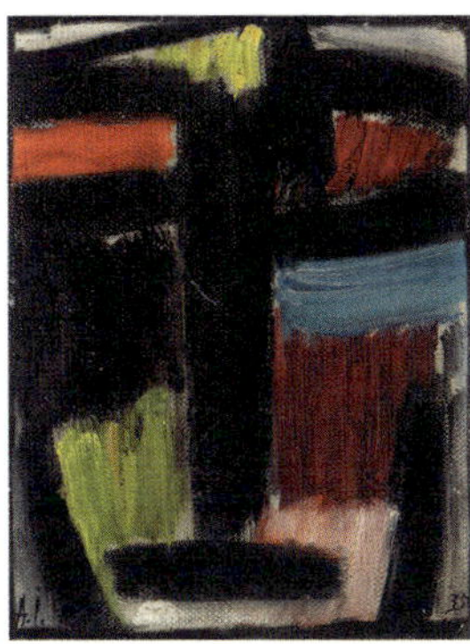 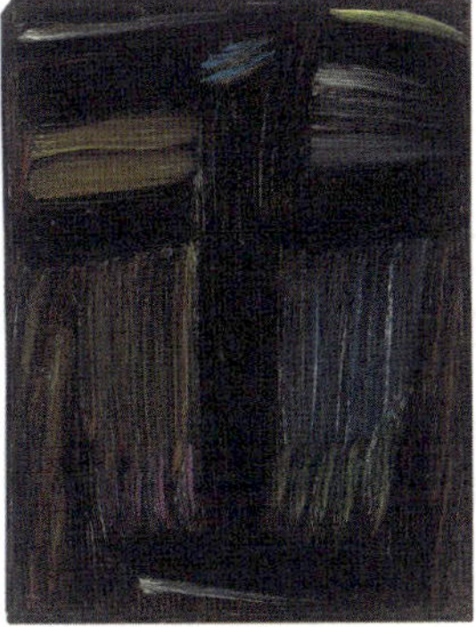 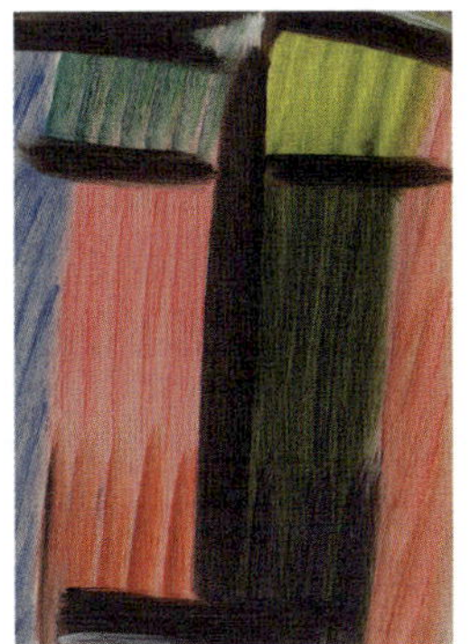

the dish of fruit that typically populates a 16th century Dutch still-life: solemn and impersonal, yet painted with a level of care and devotion that renders it capable of becoming eternal to the same degree. According to one of his early biographer's, Jawlensky's aim in this regard was far from accidental.[7] Present in the making of this work is an intrinsically religious, meditative state which Jawlensky increasingly placed himself into when producing his series, feeling his way along the contours of the space which the serial format had opened up. "I am not so much searching for new forms", he is claimed to have said, "but I want to go deeper; not to progress in breadth but in *depth*".[8] Despite their paucity of brushwork, when taken as a series the *Abstract Heads* represent a richly coloured and highly expressive body of work, wherein the overall structure of the head is retained in each. Yet the features of the face are gradually converted into geometric planes as the series progresses. As a means of systematising the syntax of the image across a number of iterations, this development allows the series to cohere as a group in a manner not dissimilar to the *Variations*. But it also means that the features of the face eventually begin to resemble vestigial forms, which prepares the way for what comes next.

3: Shirley Hopps and John Coplans, *Jawlensky and the Serial Image*, Irvine: University of California, 1966, p. 18. 4: Ibid., p. 18. 5: Ibid., p. 25. 6: John Coplans, *Serial Imagery*, Pasadena Art Museum; New York Graphic Society, 1968, p. 26. 7: Clemens Weiler, *Jawlensky: Heads, Faces, Meditations*, New York: Praeger Publishers, 1971. 8: Ibid., p. 17 (italics added).

The *Meditations* are Jawlensky's last series of heads and the culmination of his life's work. Begun in 1934 when the artist was almost crippled from advancing paralysis, the form of the head is reduced within this series to the most minimal of components. The nose appears as a single black line splitting the canvas horizontally down the middle, while the eyes and eyebrows manifest themselves as a pair of dark black strokes emerging at 45 degrees from it, cutting the canvas in crosswise fashion. Taken as a whole this configuration presents the beholder with the structure of a fixed black grid, the sensation of which is further enhanced by a series of thinner lines deployed to fill in the features of the face. These lines are applied judiciously and with colour, using strokes of varying pressure, thus allowing Jawlensky to achieve a wide degree of differentiation in the application of paint to each canvas. Although they fluctuate in terms of colour, hue and the tilt of the axis upon which the features sit, the same configuration of line and brushwork is used in each and every single *Meditation*. Yet despite such relentless repetition and formalised similarity, the *Meditations* do not appear as multiples in the manner of an edition of prints, much less as the sequential record of perceptual change upon a visible form, a la Monet. Instead the force of seriality coupled with the "cruciform framework" of pure black renders each *Meditation* as both similar to, and yet distinct from, every other *Meditation* in the series.[9] In the vestige of the face which is retained amid the repeated depiction of a place that lies elsewhere and otherwise conceived, each *Meditation* stands unique.

SERIALITY AFTER JAWLENSKY

The development of serial art continues during the 20th century and on into the 21st, although artists who successfully pursue this strategy do not achieve communion with the sublime in quite the same way, and certainly not courtesy of the human visage. In terms of audience reception, serial art reaches fruition during the heyday of

STEFANA MCCLURE
BERGMAN'S RELIGIOUS TRILOGY, 2017
GRAPHITE TRANSFER PAPER MOUNTED
ON RAG, EACH 7 × 12.7 CM
STEFANA MCCLURE STUDIO, COURTESY:
BARTHA_CONTEMPORARY, LONDON

9: Ibid., p. 18.

1960s and 1970s Minimalist and Conceptual Art, using the tools of non-pictorial abstraction then in vogue. Artists like Donald Judd, Mel Bochner, Hanne Darboven, Sol LeWitt, Eva Hesse and Dorothea Rockburne all pursue serial strategies to realise their artistic aims, with the importance of the grid and various forms of serial structure, both macro (across the series as a whole) and micro (within each individual iteration) taking centre stage. Beyond this the progress of serial art branches again, in tandem with the discursive developments taking place across contemporary art generally. One of these branches generates work that pictorially narrates the world in various ways, with artists like Florette Dijkstra and Marcel van Eeden successfully employing the structure of the series towards this end. Eeden's ongoing project *The Encyclopaedia of My Death*, consisting of drawings and other works produced in a dark and smoky film-noir aesthetic (and which relate in their entirety to source material that dates from the period before the artists birth in 1965), offers a case in point. But there are a number of other artists working today who have returned to some of the lessons on seriality learned during the 20th century. I would argue that these individuals come closer to mining the territory that Jawlensky first probed during his final years, despite the interlude of almost a century. One in particular is the contemporary artist Stefana McClure.

Conceptually McClure's oeuvre is diverse, although it pivots around a decided interest in the distillation of time and the accumulation of language. While not all her work is serial in scope, the ongoing series *Films on Paper* is the work she is perhaps best known for, and constitutes a standout example of the serial art genre. Monochromatic in form, with a spartan aesthetic redolent of the minimalist/conceptual approach, works within the *Films on Paper* series are composed of a succession of superimposed subtitles or closed captions that depict entire films, often foreign language ones, using a process of wax transfer mounted on rag. Each transcribed film often

produces a series of works that belong to it, creating serial artworks that are not only composed of micro and macro-structures, but which in turn act as a micro-structures sitting within a macro-structure (the *Films on Paper* series). For example, an artwork like *Bergman's Religious Trilogy* (2017) is both a *Films on Paper* piece and itself comprised of three small works. Named after Ingmar Bergman's famed trilogy released in the early 1960s (*Through a Glass Darkly*, *Winter Light* and *The Silence*), the subtitles of each film are visible as a pair of blurred lines located at the bottom of each. McClure's method involves tracing by hand the subtitles/captions as they appear on a screen, overlaying them as they appear in sequence. This in turn creates a sense of withdrawn or withheld depth to the finished piece: not a spatial depth, but a conceptual one, given that it emerges for the beholder only once they appreciate that the entirety of each film's dialogue is captured within the framework of two blurry lines. In the case of *Bergman's Religious Trilogy*, this sense of depth can be appreciated across all three works which make up the piece, whereupon the entire transcribed dialogue of Bergman's trilogy is appreciated as being present in the framework of six blurry lines, with all that that implies. When this realisation arises for the beholder, we have an example of what one erudite commentator aptly describes as *"serial depth"* occurring: a phenomenon unlike any other within the context of contemporary art.[10]

In the *Meditations*, Jawlensky was the first artist to establish the framework for realising such depth, one of his few stated aims. It requires the serial artwork to become a "singular plurality" rather than remain the plurality of the singular in the manner of Mondrian or Monet's series.[11] There are not many artists today who successfully manage to tread this path. Those who do, however, are rewarded with the production of a space that owes little to the physical dimensions of the work, and everything to the scope of the imagination that beholds.

Joe Graham is an artist, writer and educator with a focus on drawing research. Currently Associate Professor of Art & Design at the American University of Sharjah, UAE, he has taught interdisciplinary art & design programme in both the UK and abroad. A fine art graduate of Chelsea College of Art & Design and the Slade School of Fine Art, UCL, Graham completed his doctorate at Loughborough University with a phenomenological study of serially developed drawing. His latest publications include *Serial Drawing: Space, Time and the Art Object* (London: Bloomsbury Visual Arts, 2021) and *The Being of Drawing* (London: Marmalade Publishers of Visual Theory, 2020). For a full list of publications please see https://aus.academia.edu/JoeGraham.

10: Nicolas de Warren, "Ad Infinitum: Boredom and the Play of Imagination", in: *Infinite Possibilities: Serial Imagery in 20th-Century Drawings*. Wellesley, MA: Davis Museum and Cultural Centre, Wellesley College, 2004. pp. 1-25. Original italics. 11: Ibid., p. 9.

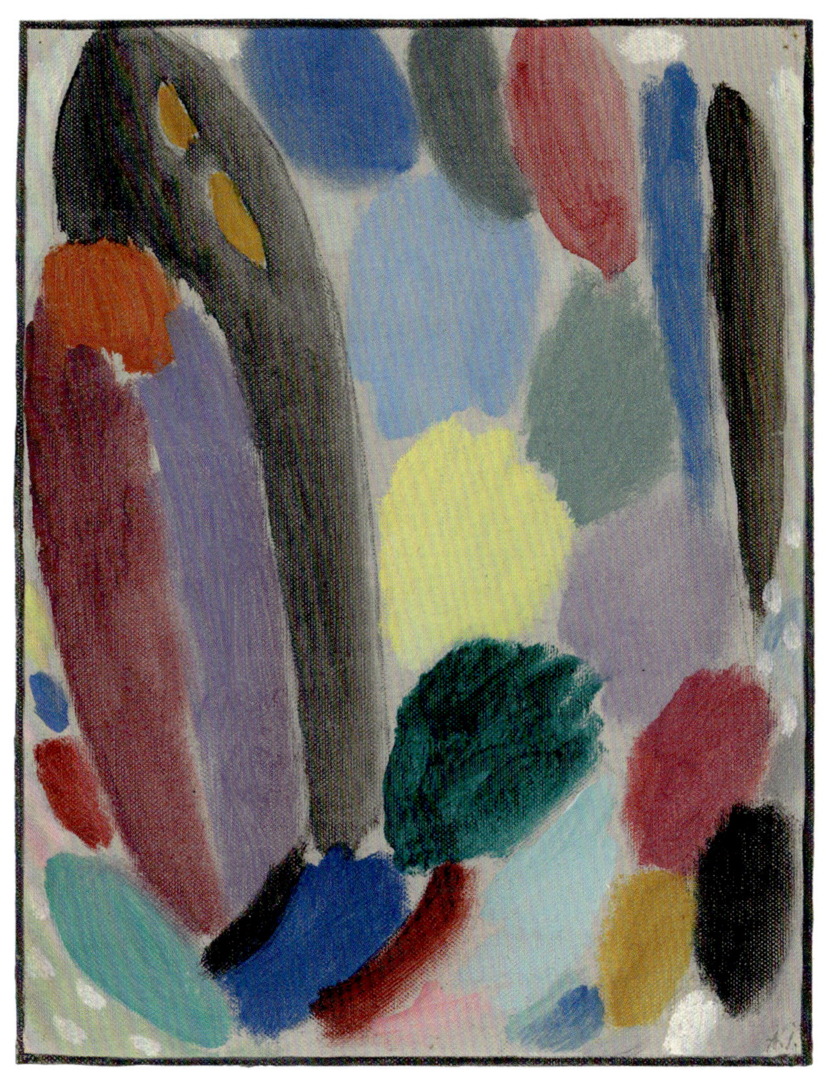

VARIATION, C. 1918

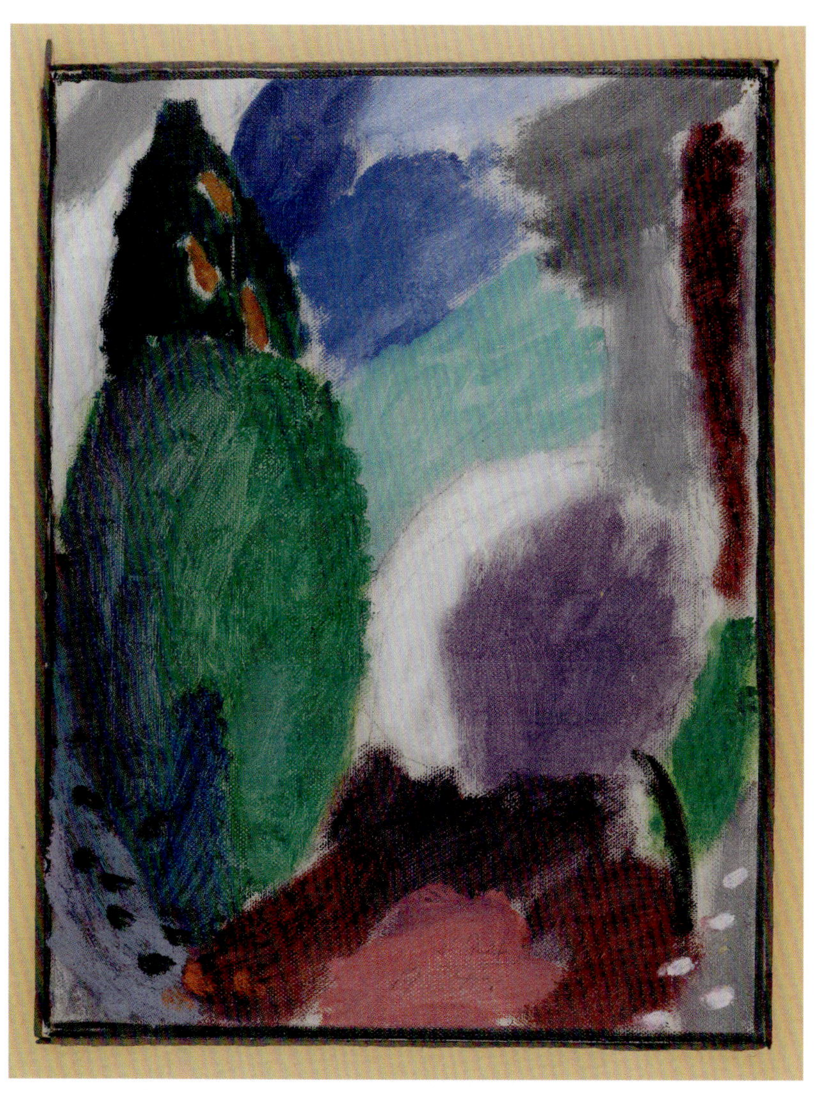

VARIATION: COLD SPRING, 1916

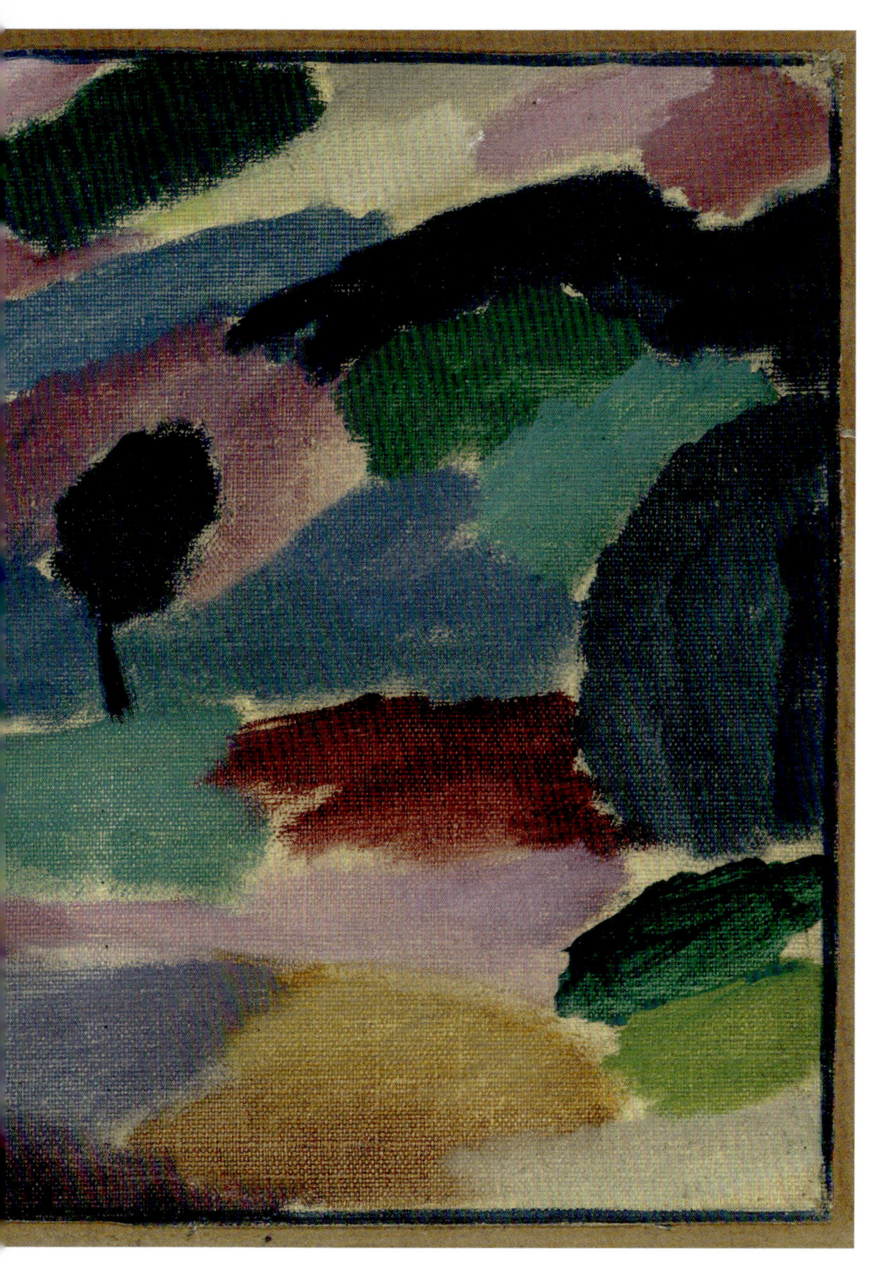

THUNDERSTORM LANDSCAPE, 1915

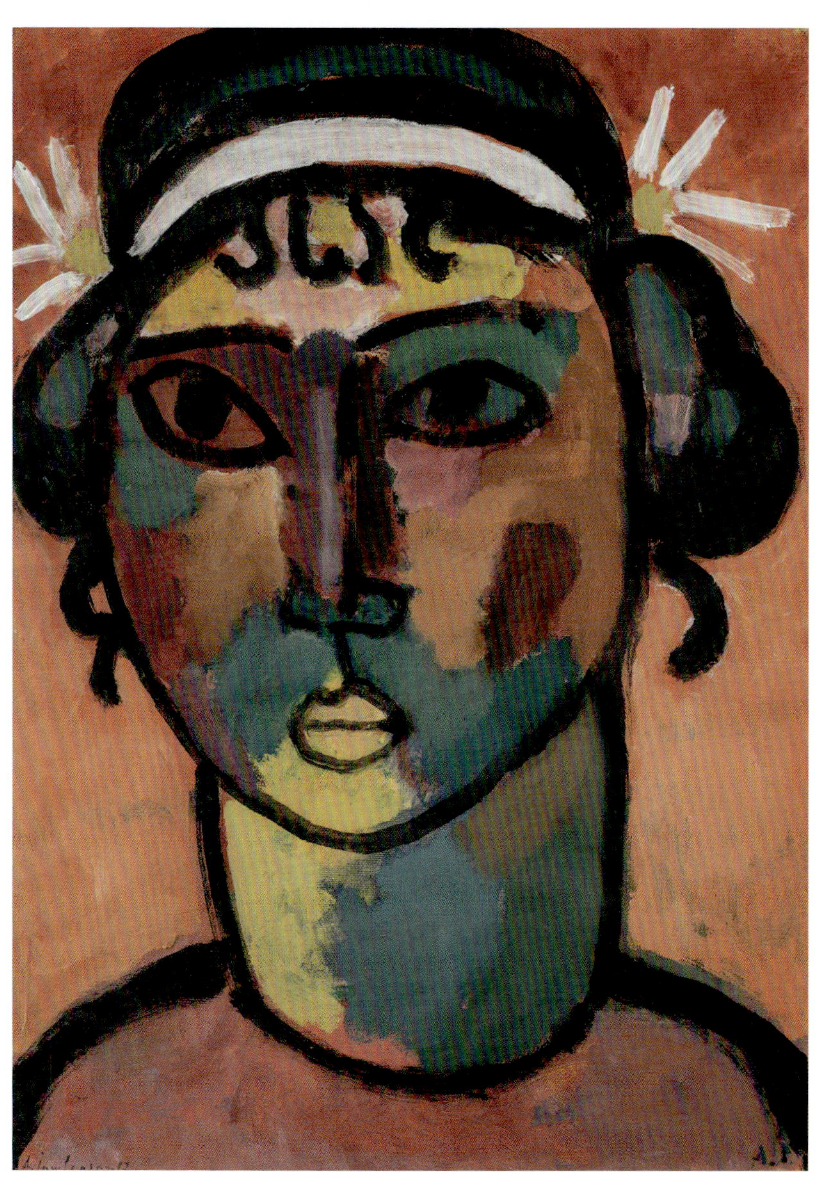

EXOTIC HEAD, 1917

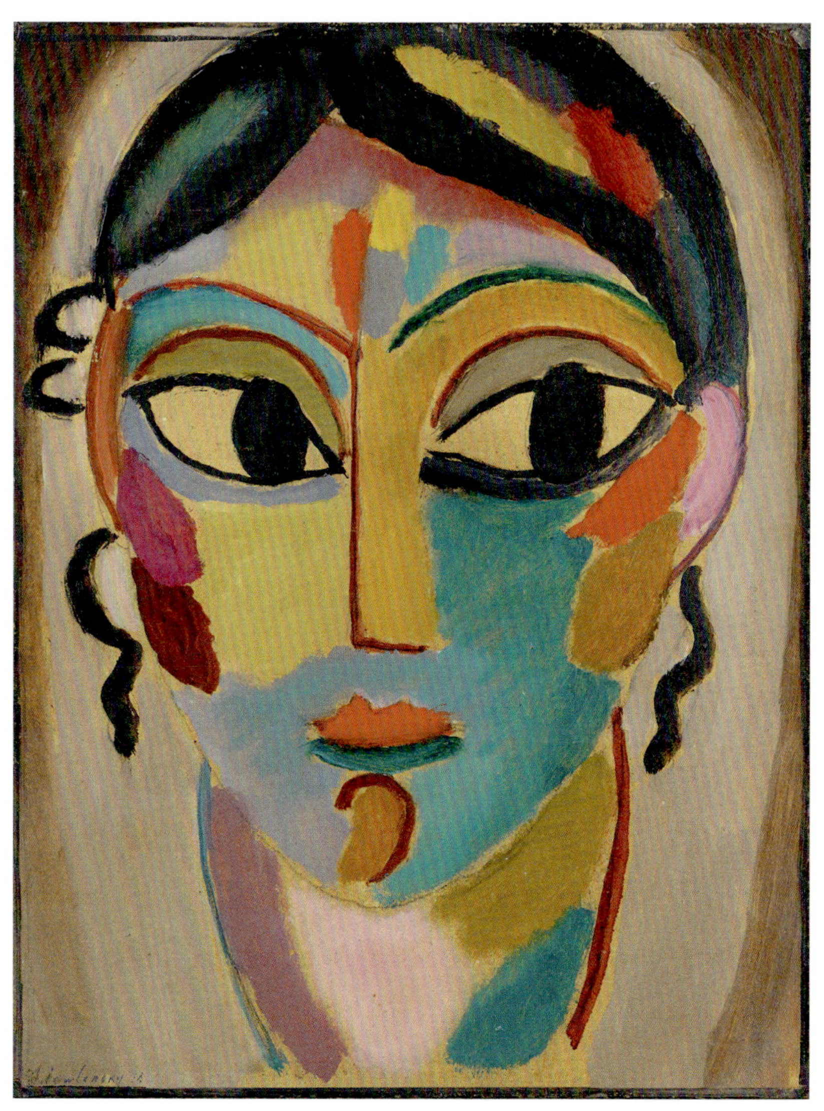

MYSTIC HEAD: GIRL'S HEAD (FRONT), 1918

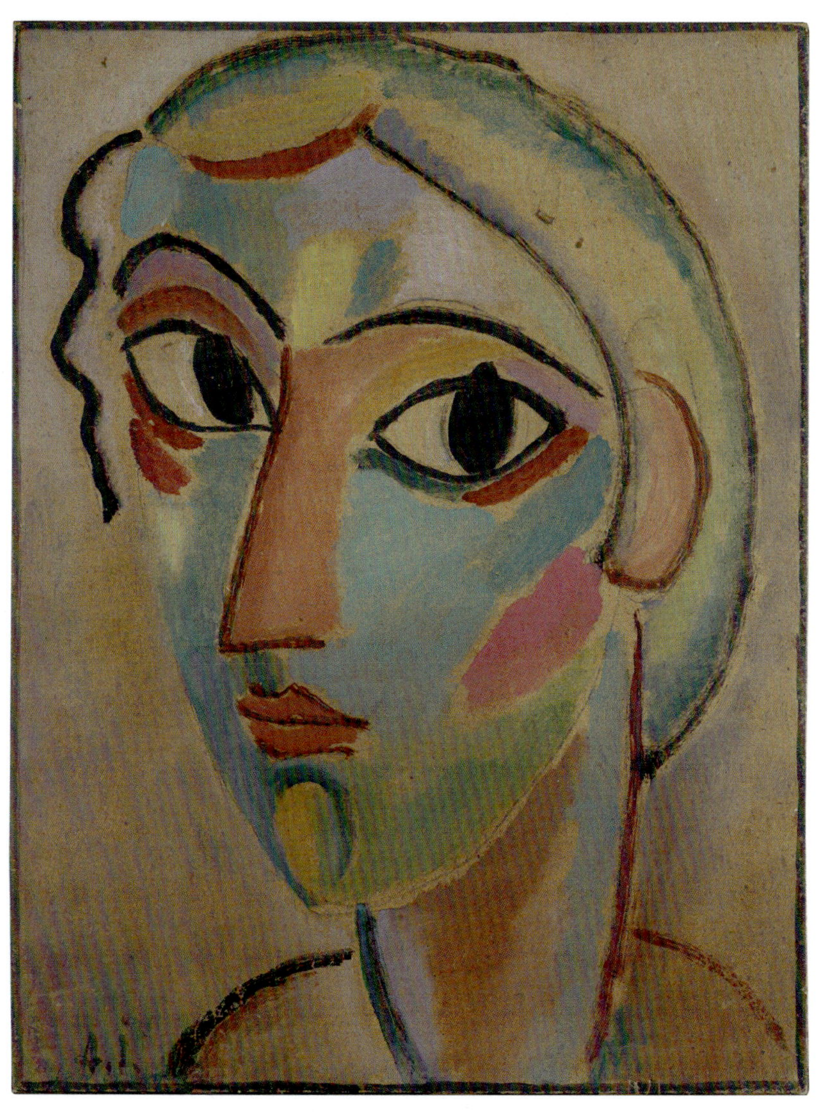

MYSTIC HEAD: GIRL'S HEAD (SLIGHTLY TURNED), 1918

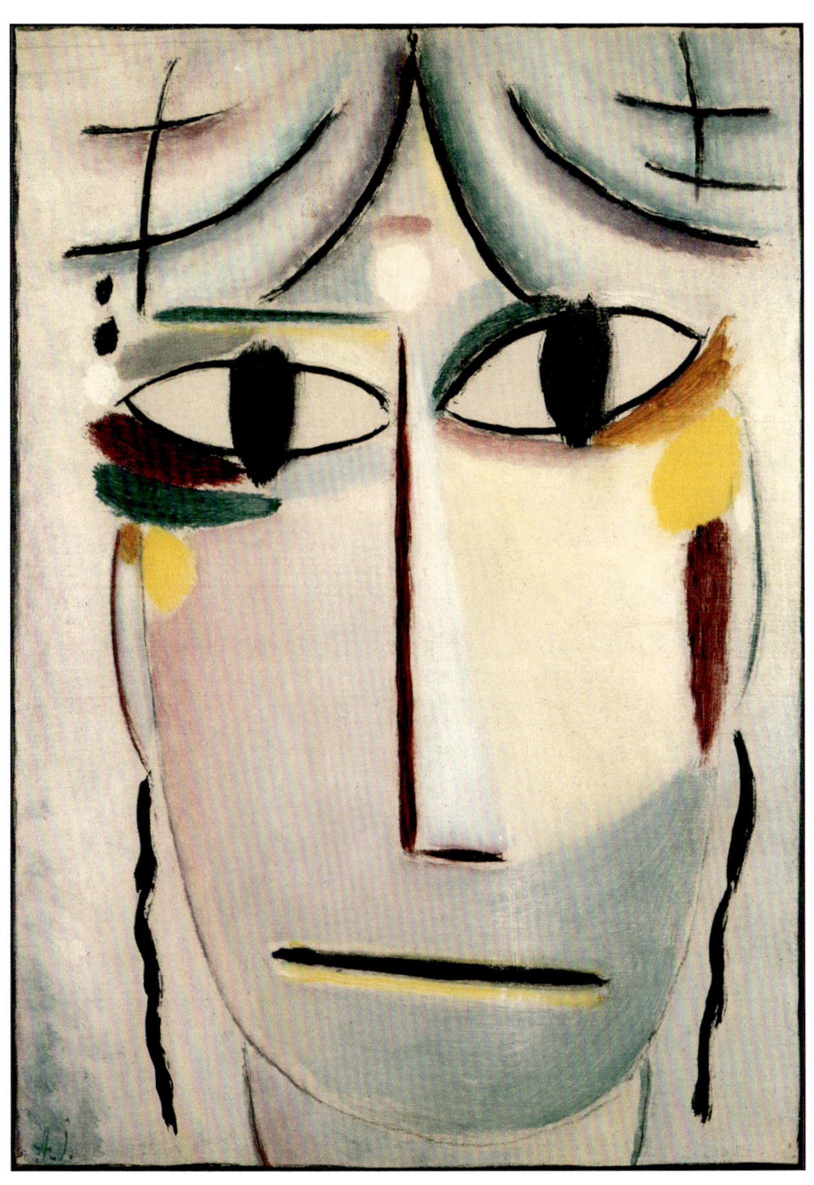

SAVIOUR'S FACE: GUARDIAN, 1920

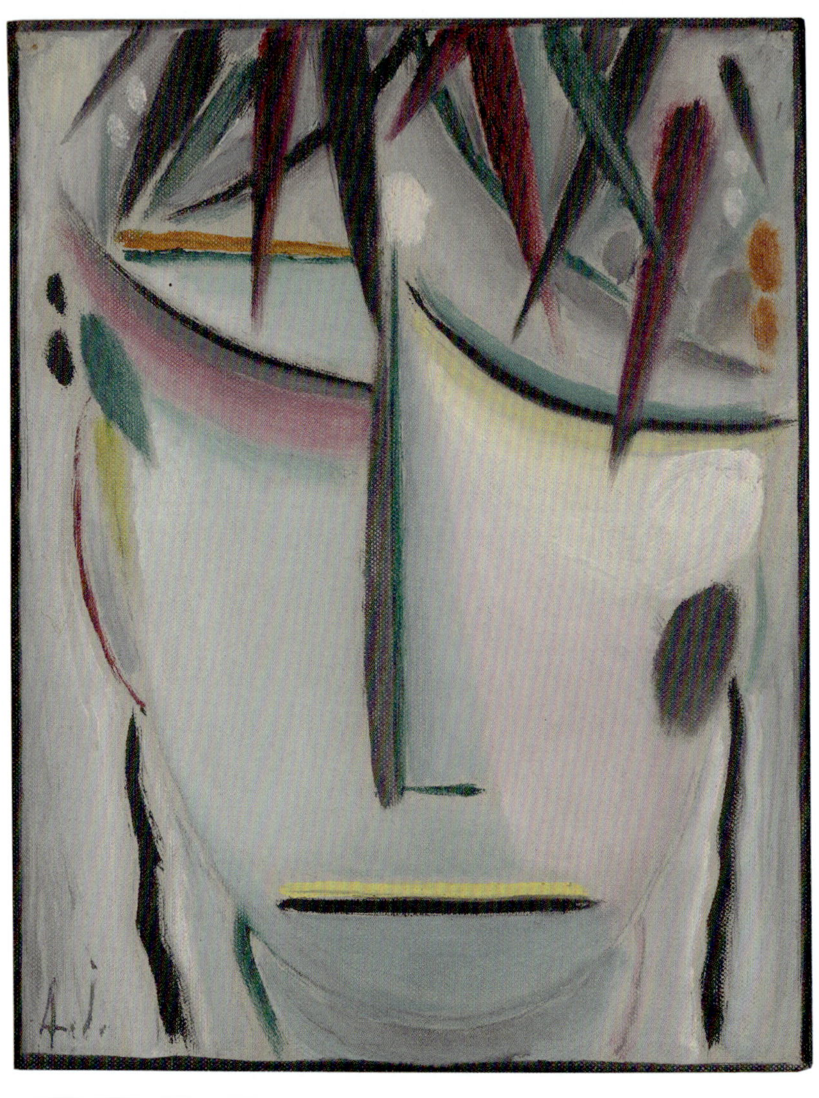

SAVIOUR'S FACE: THORNS, 1920

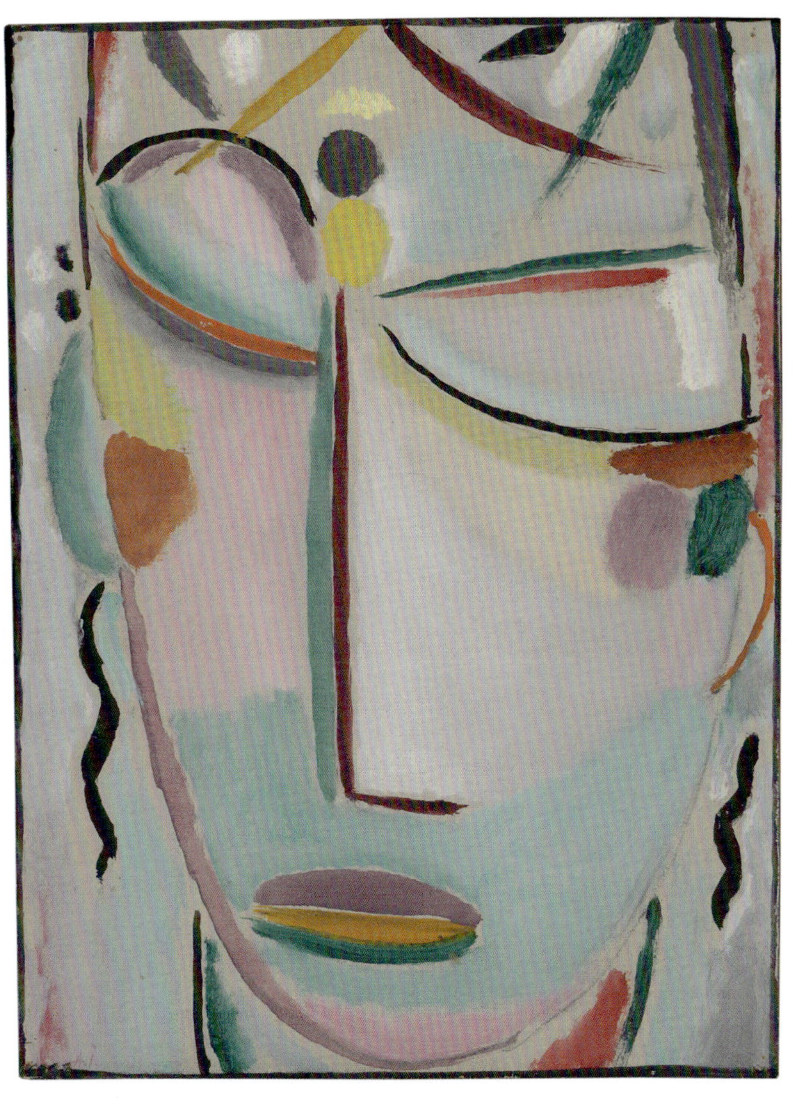

SAVIOUR'S FACE: IN LOVE, THE SPIRITUAL IS ETERNAL, 1919

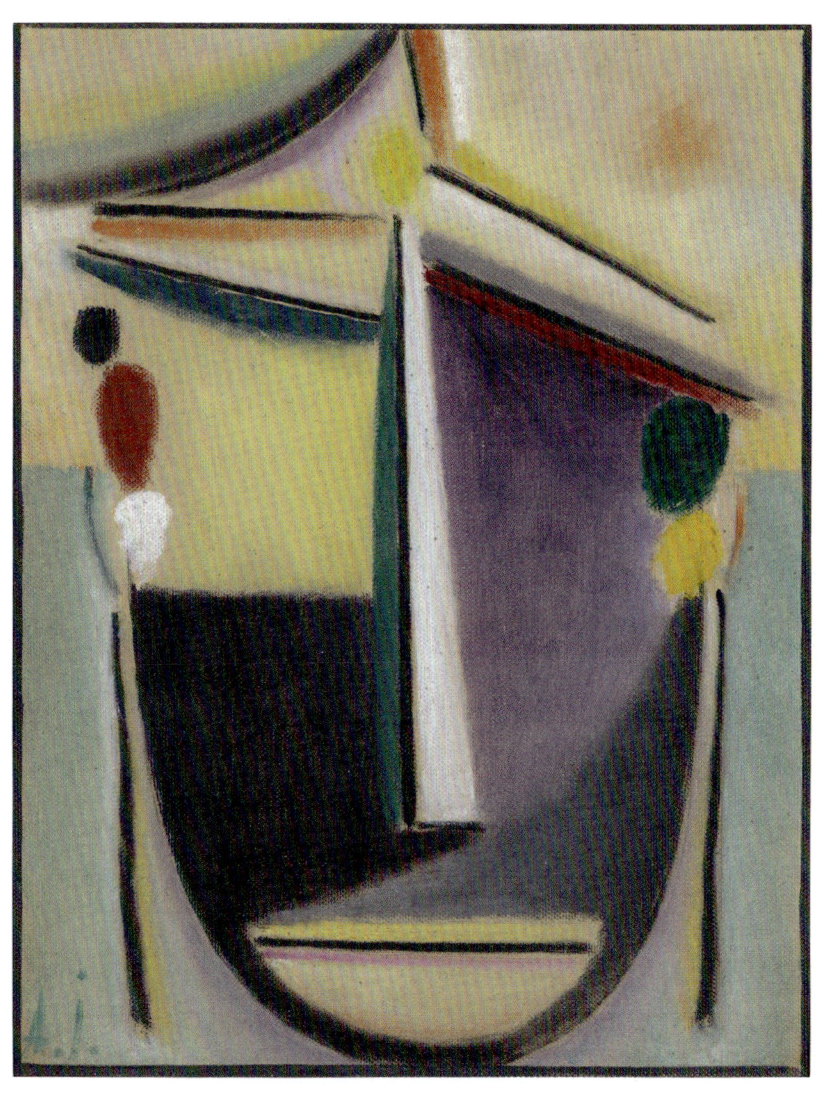

ABSTRACT HEAD: BLACK-YELLOW-PURPLE, C. 1922

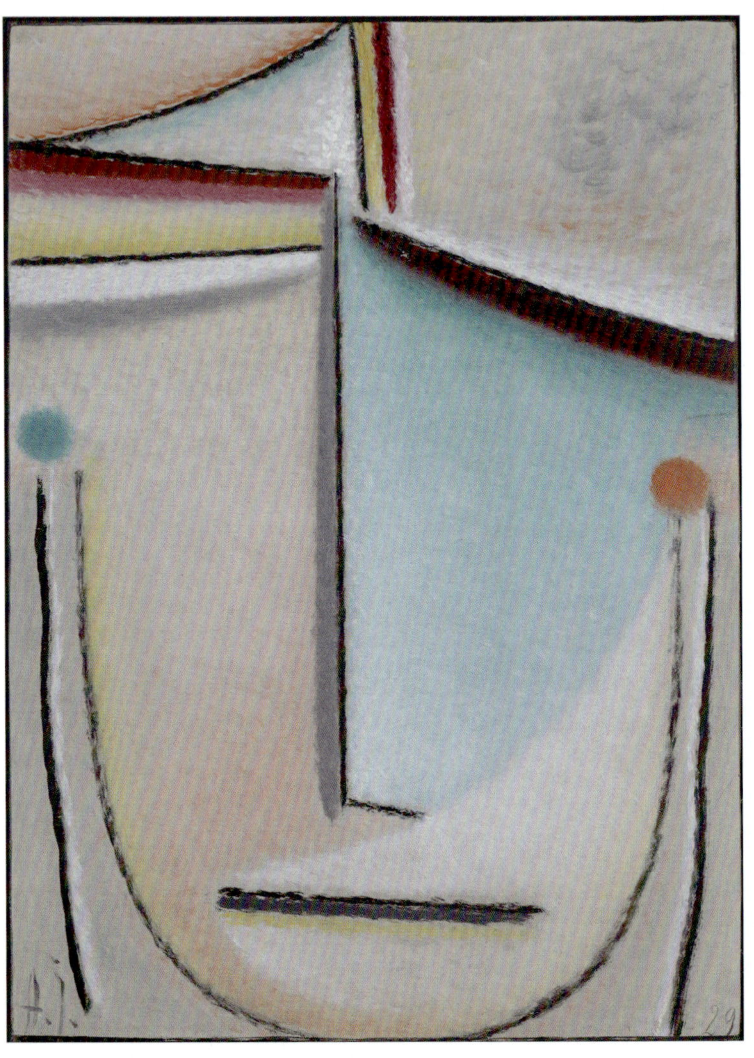

ABSTRACT HEAD: PINK-LIGHT BLUE, 1929

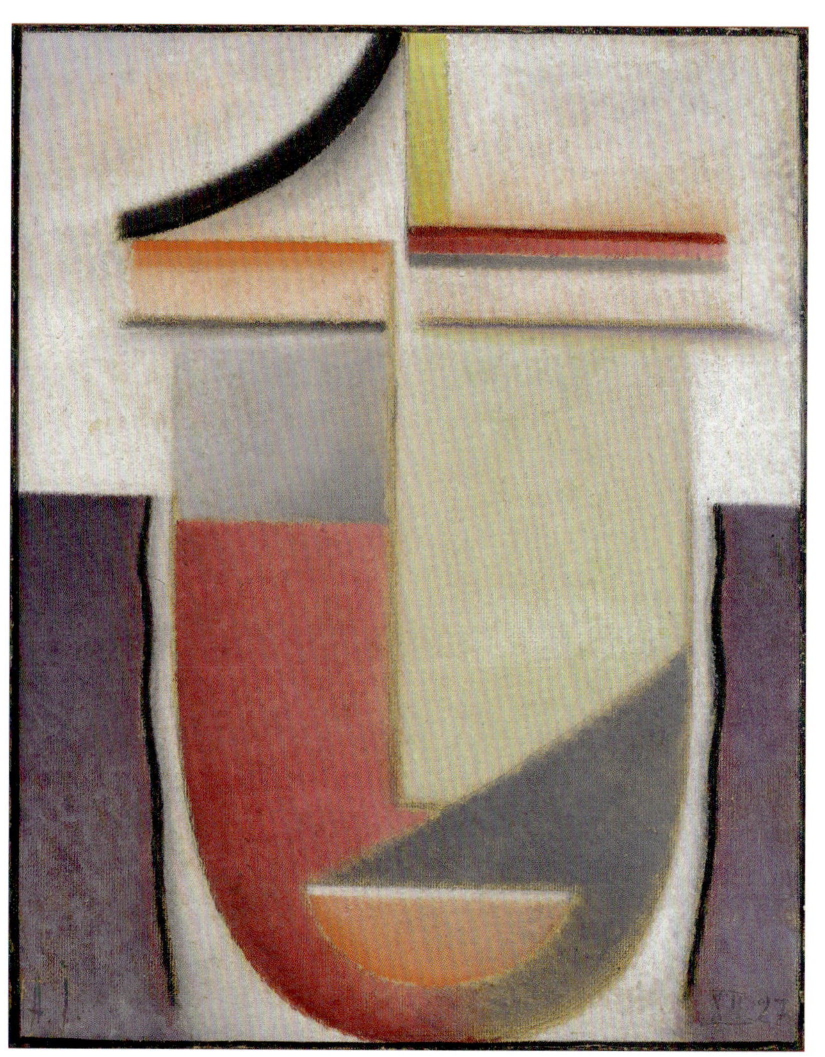

ABSTRACT HEAD: WINTER, 1927

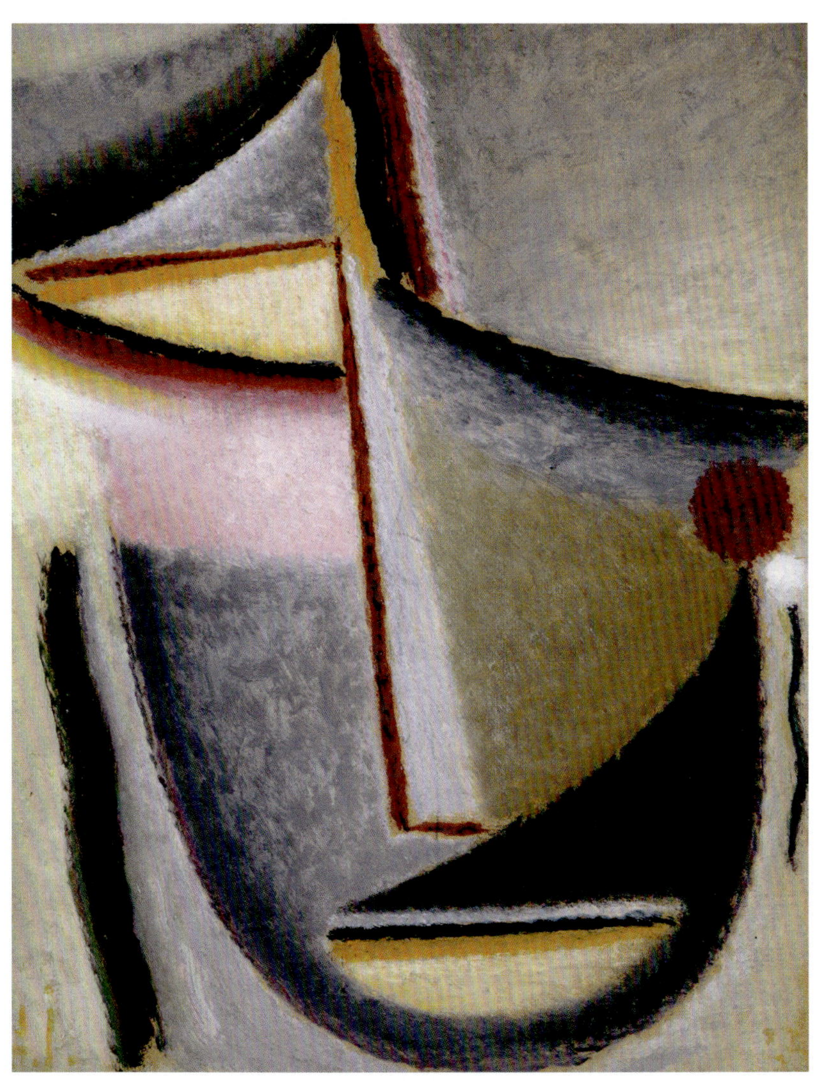

ABSTRACT HEAD (CONSTRUCTIVIST HEAD), C. 1930

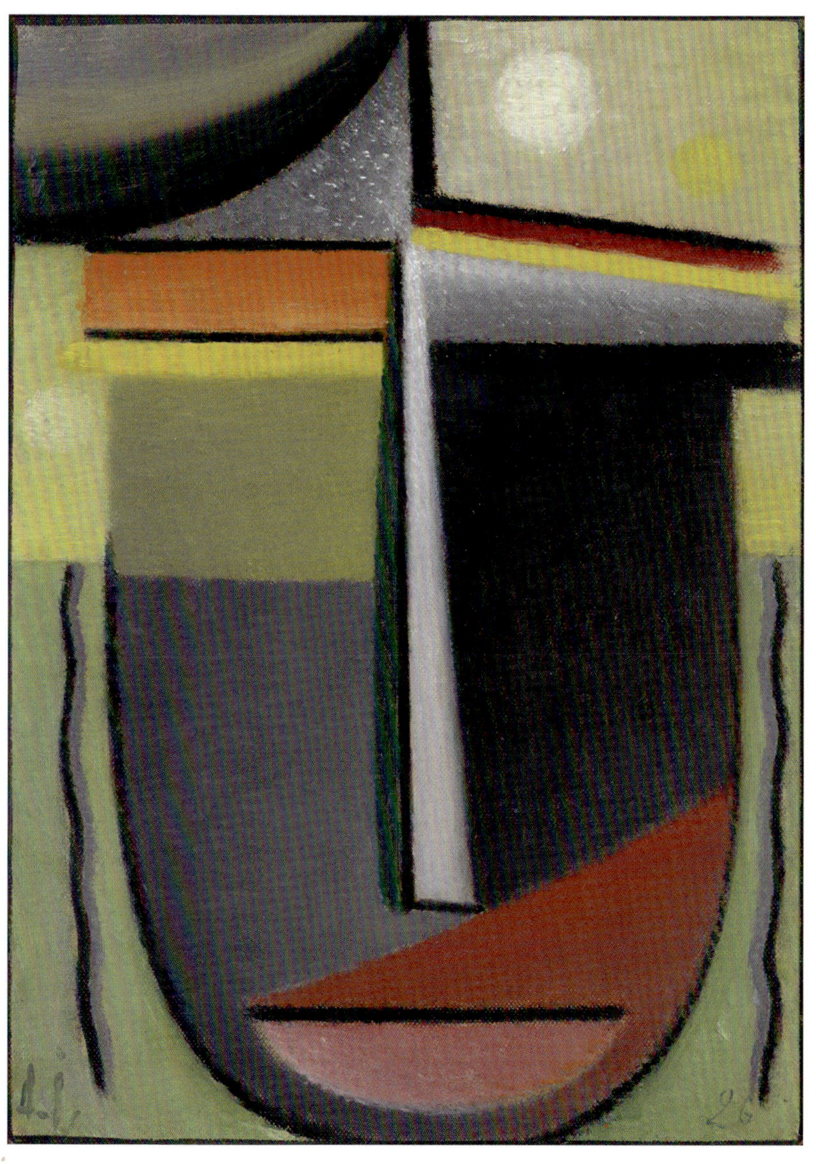

ABSTRACT HEAD: AN INNER GAZE, GOLDEN GREEN, 1926

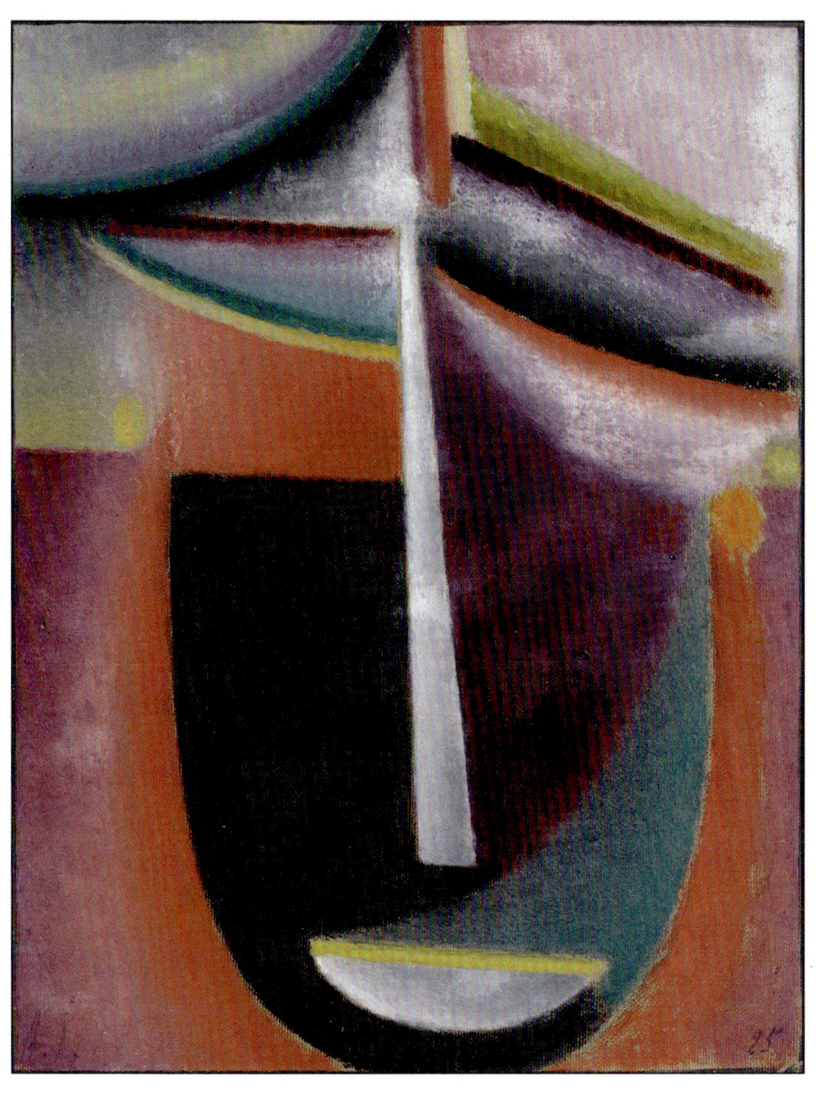

ABSTRACT HEAD: MYSTERY, 1925

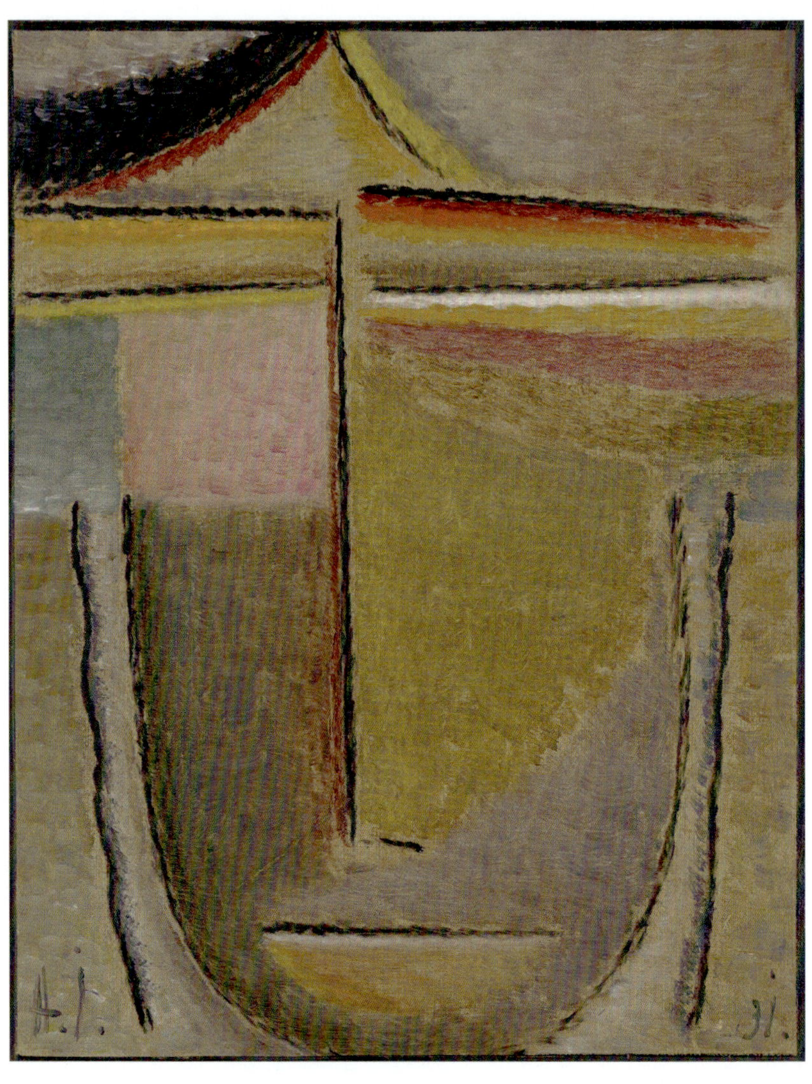

ABSTRACT HEAD: APOLLO, 1931

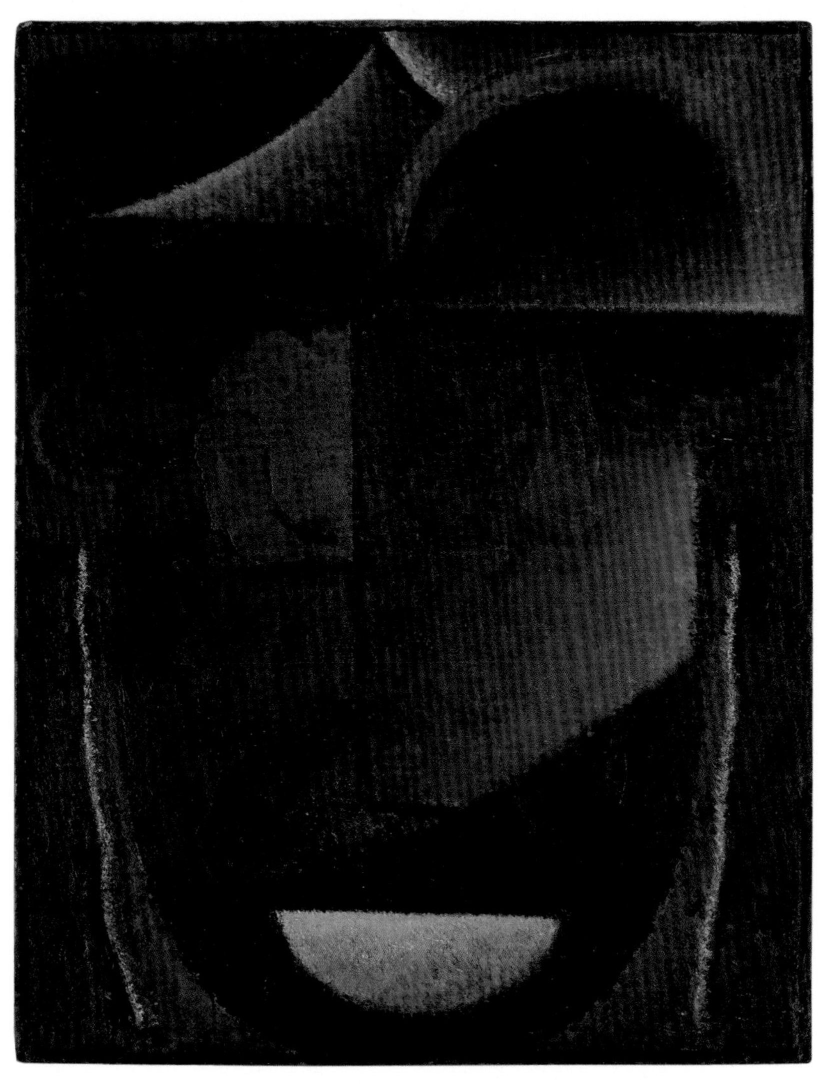

ABSTRACT HEAD: DROPS OF LIFE, 1928

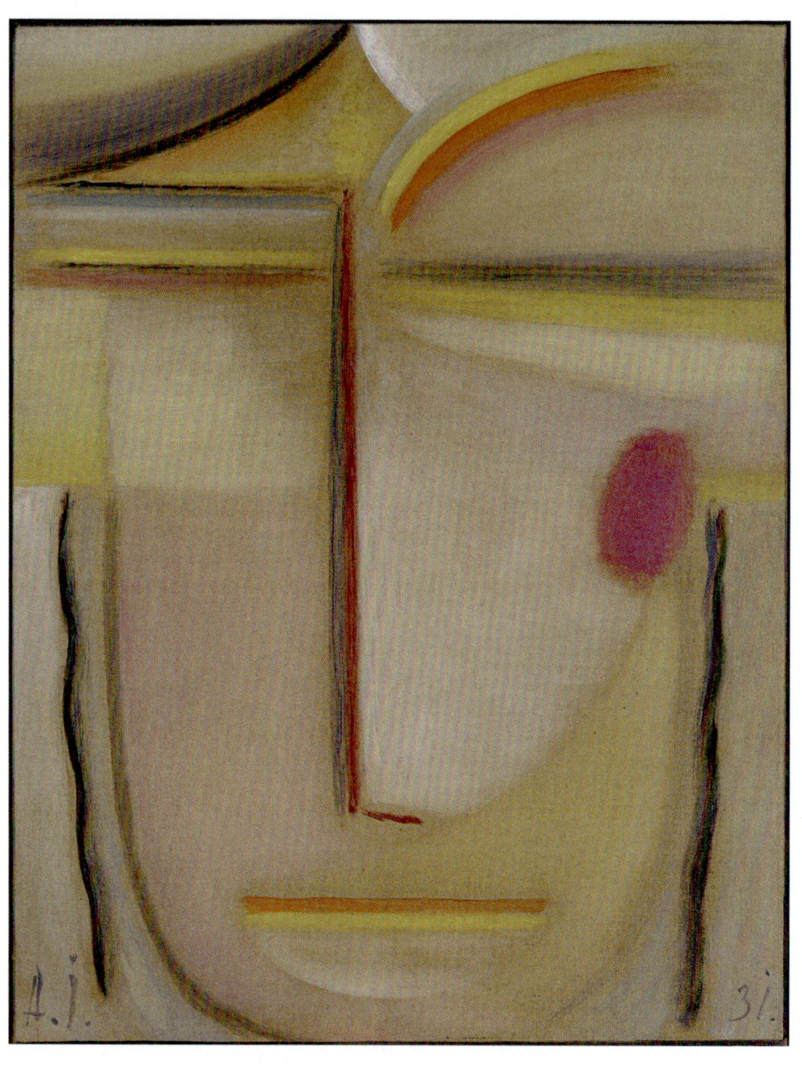

ABSTRACT HEAD: GOLD AND PINK, 1931

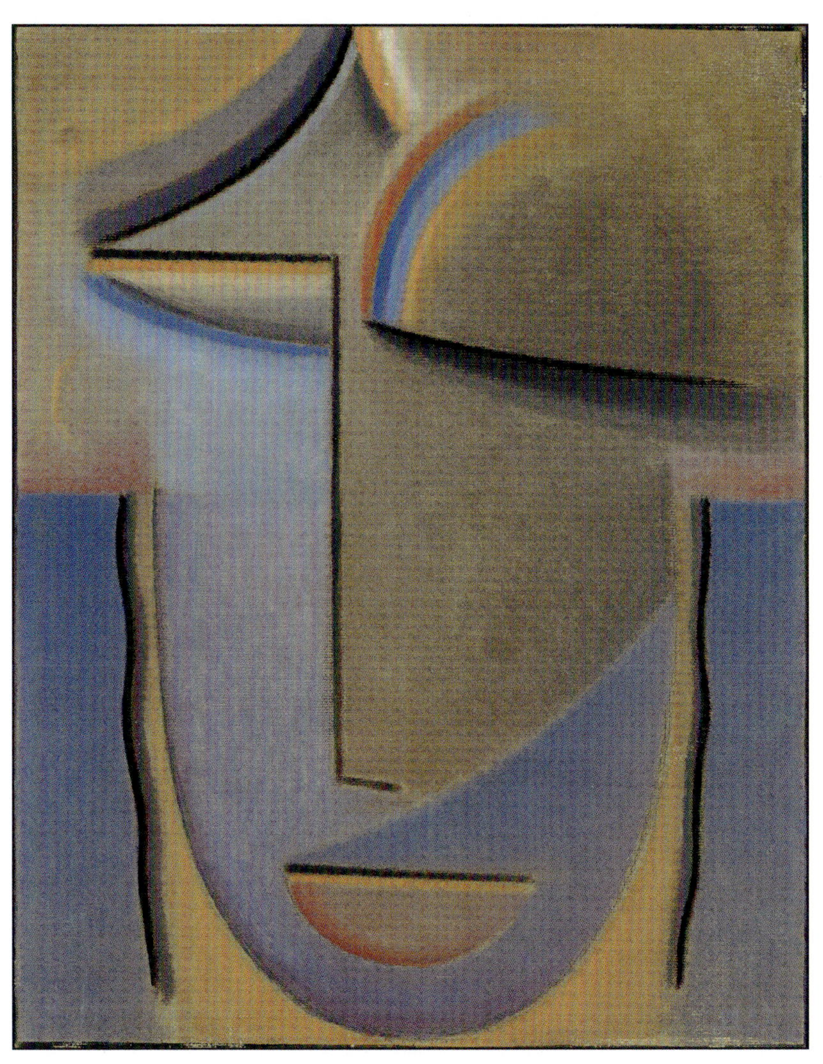

ABSTRACT HEAD: EVENING, 1927

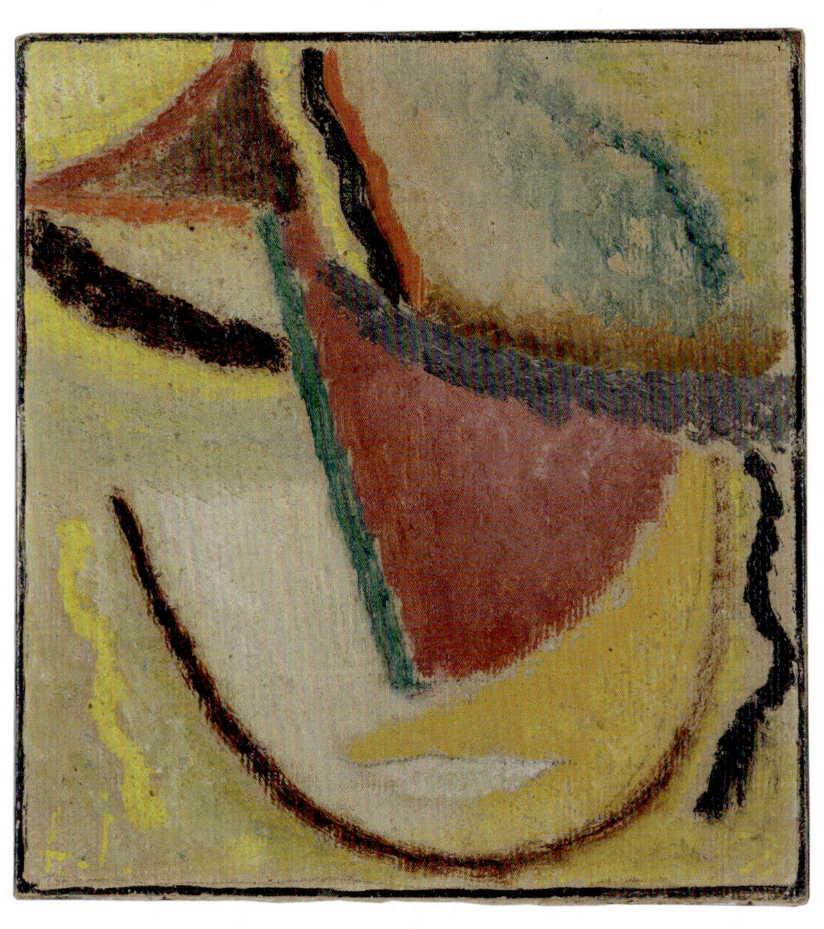

HEAD (ABSTRACT HEAD / MEDITATION), 1933

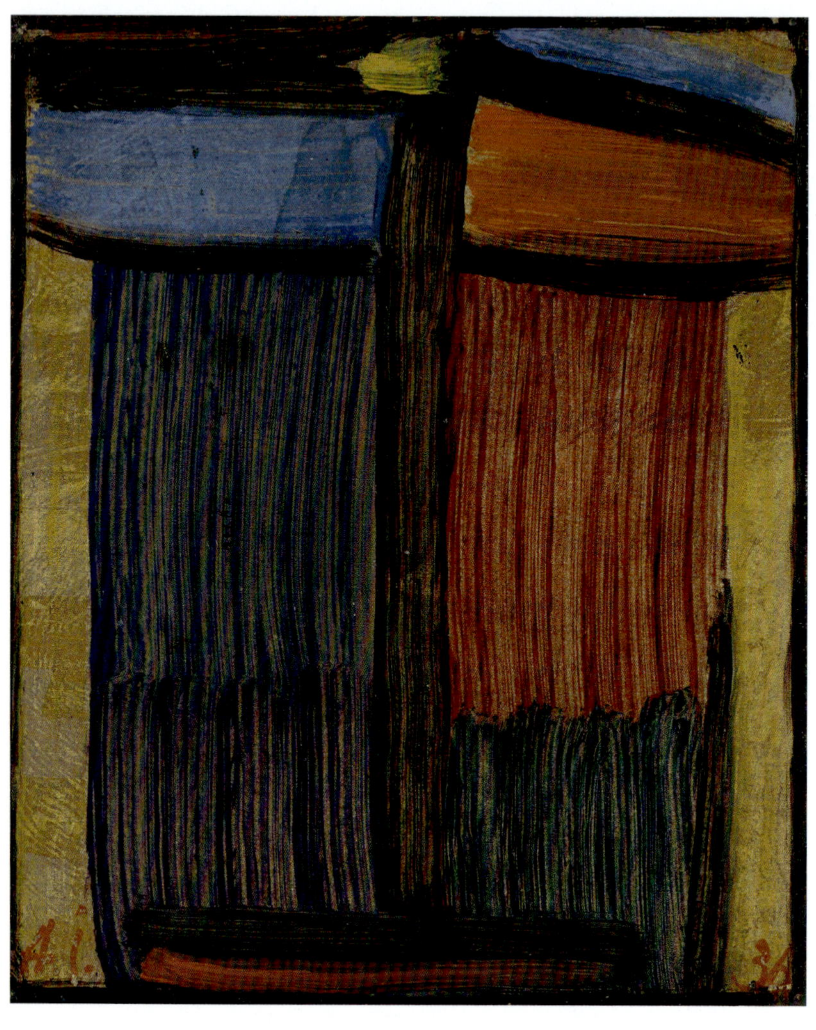

MEDITATION ON GOLDEN BACKGROUND, 1936

ALEXEJ JAWLENSKY, ICON PAINTER

BY ALEXANDER TOVBORG

The work of art is a visible God, and [...] art is "a longing for God".
For many years I did not need the prompting of nature. It was
enough for me to become absorbed within myself, to pray, and to
compose my soul in an attitude of religious devotion.
I painted many, many "Faces".
Jawlensky, 1938

Some years ago, I apprenticed with a Japanese tea master. My aim was to learn the depths of the Japanese tea ceremony, a tradition dating back to the samurai of the Edo period. Unsurprisingly, my ungainly Danish presence clashed with the minimalist serenity of a Japanese tea house, and I flunked out after just three days.

All the same, one of the many things I took with me, including in my painting, was the tea master's instruction to "Grip the tea cup, so it knows what you want with it." The idea of having a clear direction before you paint, before you even pick up the brush, heightens everything, creating a beautiful drama of painter, colours, brush and canvas. Jawlensky, I believe, had a similar approach.

I
THE POWER OF ICONS

Writing an icon. This is the correct term for when a believer paints an icon. So called because one literally paints a prayer. In the modern Western pictorial tradition, both of these phrases seem paradoxical, even impossible. To understand how painting and prayer are united, we need to turn to Orthodox Catholic iconolatry.

The power of icons stems from believers considering icons a gateway directly into, or up to, the divine. The Russian artist Alexej Jawlensky was born into this cultural acceptance of mystery and religion. In his memoirs, he describes his first encounter with an icon. Visiting a Polish church, he watched as a Madonna was theatrically revealed behind a golden curtain to the sound of trumpets, while the congregation praised and beseeched the icon, which was said to perform miracles. Encountering this icon, known as the Black Madonna of Częstochowa, was seminal for Jawlensky. It sparked his artistic calling, which was arguably religious in nature. Indeed, the mystery and power of images was never absent from the artist's understanding of images, even after he left Russia at the age of 32.

Jawlensky's faith in images, and in worship through images, is most clearly evident in his final two series of works, *Abstract Heads* and *Meditations*. The works are akin to icons in their small dimensions and methodical repetition of the portrait motif. Within the academic tradition of painting, icons are considered a school of portraiture, in the same vein as Jawlensky's practice during the last two decades of his life.

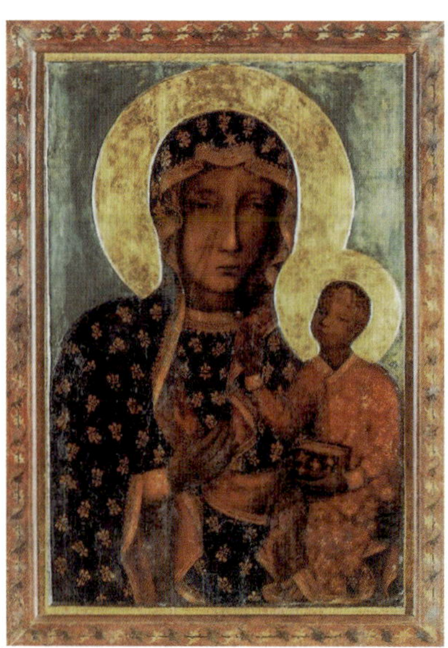

II

PORTRAIT PAINTER

In 1914, Jawlensky had yet to embark on his big project, but he was on his way. His focus was not on people. Looking out of his window at nature, he produced a series of beautiful paintings that can be seen as a conceptual preamble to his later works. *Variations*, he called these painterly and spiritual meditations on nature.

Through the artist's eye, we see woods, a path and the sky, a view he repeated over and over again in lush variations. Then suddenly, something happened to both the colours and the subject. The whole spatial understanding of nature dissolved, to the point where the viewer has to squint to see nature in his paintings. Jawlensky pushes the viewer to the point where realism has to be relinquished to grasp what is what in the paintings.

Jawlensky meditated daily, and it seems reasonable to assume that he used nature as his visual and spiritual anchor. Woods, path and sky make up his internal meditation image. Just as the stages of meditation can lead to a state of relaxation or focus, Jawlensky's nature paintings from this period have the character of an internal landscape, of a state of flow more than any particular place.

This exploration of internal images came to define Jawlensky's later work. The series marks the first appearance of Jawlensky's distinctive artistic voice. Through repetition, he was studying not only landscape but also his own style. He articulates trees and skies with his palette. His brushstrokes get increasingly bigger. Trees fuse with landscape. Reality becomes a construct. The more landscapes he paints, the further Jawlensky seems to get from the actual nature before him.

III

THE MADONNA

With few exceptions, all icons are portraits. The most famous is undoubtedly the one known today as the Madonna. This icon shows the Virgin Mary with the baby Jesus, who often looks older than his infant years. The Madonna motif exists in a fascinating array of beautiful versions. Other well-known icon portraits include John the Baptist, Saint Nicholas and, a favourite of mine, the face of Jesus on Veronica's veil.

My private collection of icons includes many deteriorated Russian icons, most made around the time of the Russian Revolution in 1917, during Jawlensky's life. Under Communism, icons suffered. As the regime sought to dismantle the Church, Soviet officials sold off everything from crosses to gilded church interiors and icons. This is one reason why there are more icons in Europe today than remain in

Russia. Over the years, many icons have been bought back, although there are still major collections in Denmark, both in private hands and at Sorø Art Museum, which is definitely worth a visit.

The French painter Henri Matisse (1869-1954) was a collector of icons. What little information is available about this minor but vital chapter on the artist states that he did not collect *attractive* but *good* icons. He was reportedly not interested in an icon's condition or history but solely in its unique painterly qualities.

I have acquired my icons at auction and in antique shops, most of them are Madonnas – it was also a Madonna that captivated Jawlensky at his first art experience. Familiar and archetypal, the image of a mother and child holds universal power.

After the birth of my daughter in 2020, I began to ponder why all Madonnas are alike. Perhaps the motif of the mother and son is no longer au courant? I wanted to open up the image and replace Jesus with a girl child, make the Madonna more relevant. Like Jawlensky, who worked in series of the same motif, I have explored the Madonna motif in my own paintings since 2021, spinning off independent versions and whole new interpretations of the icon.

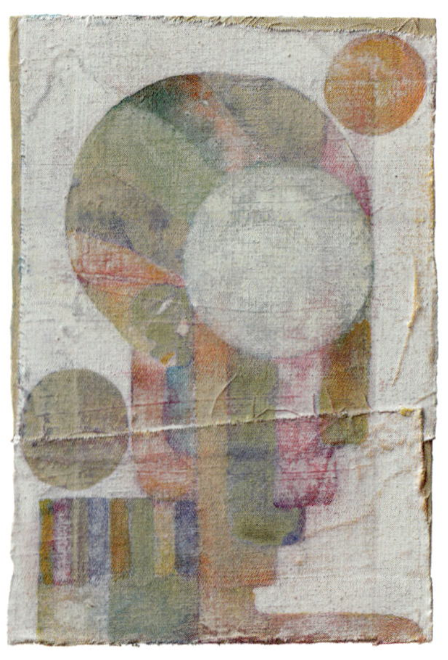
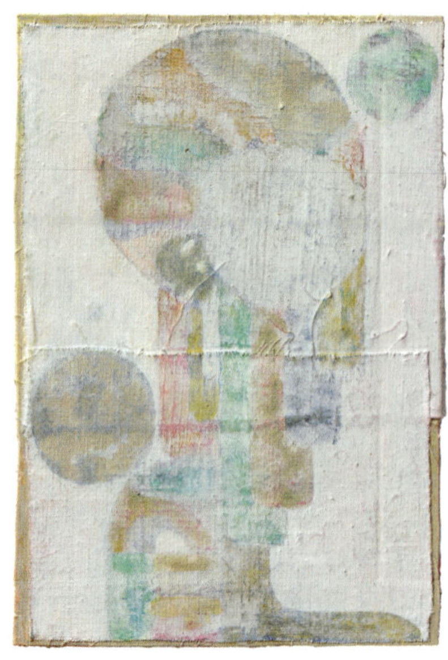

The Vatican keeps a long list of Catholically-approved Madonnas. There is a Madonna for virtually everything – one for families, one for untangling knots and another for people who live in the jungle. Inspired by the Vatican's canonised list, I did an exhibition of new Madonnas in 2022. I painted a *Madonna of Longing* for those I missed and a *Madonna of the Coin* for those who might be struggling financially. Recently, I added an *Astronaut Madonna*. The idea of humanity leaving the planet and venturing into the cosmos, to escape or out of curiosity, could have come straight out of Dante's *Divine Comedy* and its journey to Paradise.

IV
ABSTRACT HEAD

Icons and Jawlensky's final two series of works have in common that they are portraits. Jawlensky's paintings, however, stand in notable contrast to the tradition of iconography, since his portraits, unlike icons, are not of any particular person. The portraits lack pronouns and are simply titled *Kopf* (Head). Whether a specific person is being portrayed seems to be of secondary importance to him. "Head", presumably, is nonspecific. He was striving to achieve a more universal, timeless portrait of humanity.

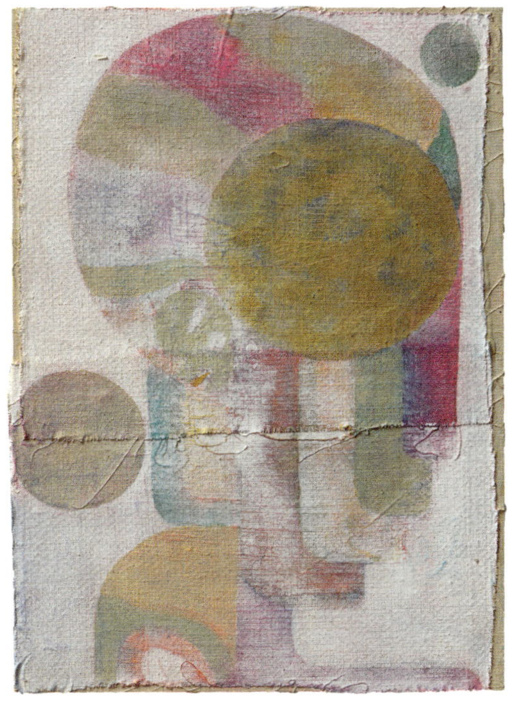

Moreover, in contrast to Western art history's long list of celebrated geniuses, the icon tradition places much less emphasis on individual artistic performance, and the notion of idolising famous painters is far less pronounced. Interestingly, even today, icon painting is still generally considered a mere craft, even though it also constitutes religious and spiritual labour.

Here, between the polar extremes of sacred and profane, we must navigate carefully to study Jawlensky's mystical icon paintings. In the last two decades of his life, Jawlensky, with one or two exceptions, devoted himself to portrait painting. The motif of the head would seem to have been enough for him – and of course, we might glibly add, we all have a head. The head symbolises human thought and per-ception. In our heads, we gather and process knowledge and impres-sions. But is it even possible to portray an abstract head? This seems as paradoxical as "writing a picture", which is precisely what Jawlensky was doing in his final series of works. The eyebrows and nose are indi-cated by the letter T, while the nose by itself is marked by an L.

When I was very little, my grandmother, who otherwise claimed that she could only draw the back of a cow, taught me my first portrait by this simple rhyme: "Full stop, full stop, comma, dash – that's how you draw Nikolaj" (in Danish, it rhymes). It might seem blasphemous to mention this nursery rhyme in the same breath as Alexej Jawlensky, but add a T and you have a rough lettering manual for Jawlensky's *Head* paintings, which once again underscores the connection be-tween writing an icon and Jawlensky's paintings.

The T in the artist's paintings is a cross simplified into a character. Picture a cross in the middle of your face, or even as your face itself. Some might find that beautiful, others too violent. But perhaps the viewer should experience it in both ways at once. The T is both a cross and pure shape: two lines. It is everything and nothing, and most of all a forehead.

By this point, Jawlensky had developed a conceptual form, a picto-rial writing template defined by repeated elements. In the 1930s, Jawlensky was not only meditating, he was exploring and expanding his practice and process. Looking at his paintings, we see the cross-like T as eyebrows and nose, the L as a nose, circles and dots as eyes, and suns or moons as fixed focal points. These are all symbols, but at the same time they are just lines and dots, pure form. The focus is sustained in the written characters, while everything around them varies. In the West, this style is called Modernism. Jawlensky's friend and fellow artist Paul Klee (1879-1940) is worth mentioning here be-cause he also worked with letters and characters, erasing the bound-ary between form and meaning in his divinely beautiful paintings.

MEDITATIONS

Alongside his Christian faith, Jawlensky practiced yoga and meditation. Bear in mind, this was the 1920s (and 1930s), not the 2020s. This kind of spirituality was not widely practiced at the time. Meditation equals clarity, focus and precision. Indeed, the artist's last series of works – like *Abstract Heads*, they are small icon-like portraits – was titled *Meditations*.

The artist-monk Fra Angelico reportedly said a prayer while mixing colours for his famous frescoes (1438-1450) in the San Marco church in Florence. This seems plausible, since prayer, by its nature, is inward meditation seeking an outward connection. In the Christian tradition, prayer is aimed at something bigger – God, the Virgin Mary or the Holy Spirit.

A prayer can be a recited text or an improvisation. In contemporary terms, it could be likened to leaving a voicemail after an unanswered call. Prayer is a mode of speech in which the supplicant addresses someone or something. Speaking or thinking a prayer out loud establishes the connection to the divine. Prayer is communicated in two directions – inward, and outward to the divine.

As a side note, I can mention the time I met the Virgin Mary in Amager, Copenhagen, in 2018. I encountered her through a medium able to connect with the spiritual realm so profoundly that they became possessed by the Holy Mother of God, a state brought about by deep meditation. I conversed with the Virgin Mary as the most natural thing in the world, and was allowed to ask a question: How did she feel about the way that she and her child had been used to unite generations and nations, but also abused by the Church in imperialist and geopolitical power struggles and warfare? Mary replied that, looking out at a crowd of people, it quickly becomes apparent that everyone has their own understanding and interpretation of the Bible. Some worship God in love, others out of greed.

VI
THE PRACTICE OF REPETITION

Like most Western painters, Jawlensky worked in oils. He was a painter with a capital P. Judging by the sheer volume of his paintings, he was obsessed. My painting idol Ursula Reuter Christiansen would call this kind of painter a *Malerschwein* (a painter pig).

At first glance, Jawlensky seems to be somersaulting from one painting to the next in a spirit of tireless playfulness. Closer examination reveals the immense persistence and discipline inherent in his practice. Jawlensky must surely have led an incredibly structured daily life, giving him a continual sense of direction from one work to the next. This could only be achieved through relentless activity – both in painting and in mental preparation.

Repetition plays a major role in the making, cultivation and understanding of images. Indeed, through repetition, an image can become so familiar that it comes to represent an ideal – in the case of the Virgin and Child, the mother taking care of the child, and the child being a boy. Over time, through repetition and dissemination, this becomes structurally embedded, perpetuating the cultivation not only of the Virgin and Child but of the concept of patrimony.

As a painter, I, too, have worked with repetitions of motif, colour and scale. My introduction to the device of repetition came through Christian iconolatry in Europe. As a child, I remember being vaguely disappointed that all churches had similar altarpieces and crosses. Why were they all the same? The answer was, because it's important. By and by, the idea of the power of repetition was implanted in me, and I continue to work with and against it.

Repetition of motifs is a big and essential part of the production of religious images. Like pop culture, the church has always been a massive producer of images. Since its inception, the institution has produced and disseminated signs, symbols, metaphors and allegories for the masses. The vast body of work which broadly constitutes Western art history has appealed to people but has also held us captive for centuries, while laying the mythological foundation for the visual mediation engaged in today on social media platforms like Instagram and TikTok.

VII
DARKNESS

During his final years, Jawlensky's palette grew darker. Perhaps his illness made him acutely aware of his mortality. Where previously his paintings radiated light, he seemed to be left with only the light of a candle, painting until the final flicker. His last works are captivating and touching in so many ways, while, in their rough paint handling and deep, dark tones, they ask a lot of the viewer. They are like turning off the light and adjusting to the darkness. Like closing your eyes and meditating to see clearly.

Alexander Tovborg is a Danish artist whose practice explores ancient symbolism and storytelling. Through his layered and labor-intensive techniques, he has created a visual language that runs throughout the work, spanning different series, figures and motives. His works are included in prominent collections such as the Hammer Museum in Los Angeles, USA, Moderna Museet in Stockholm and ARoS Aarhus Art Museum in Aarhus, Denmark.

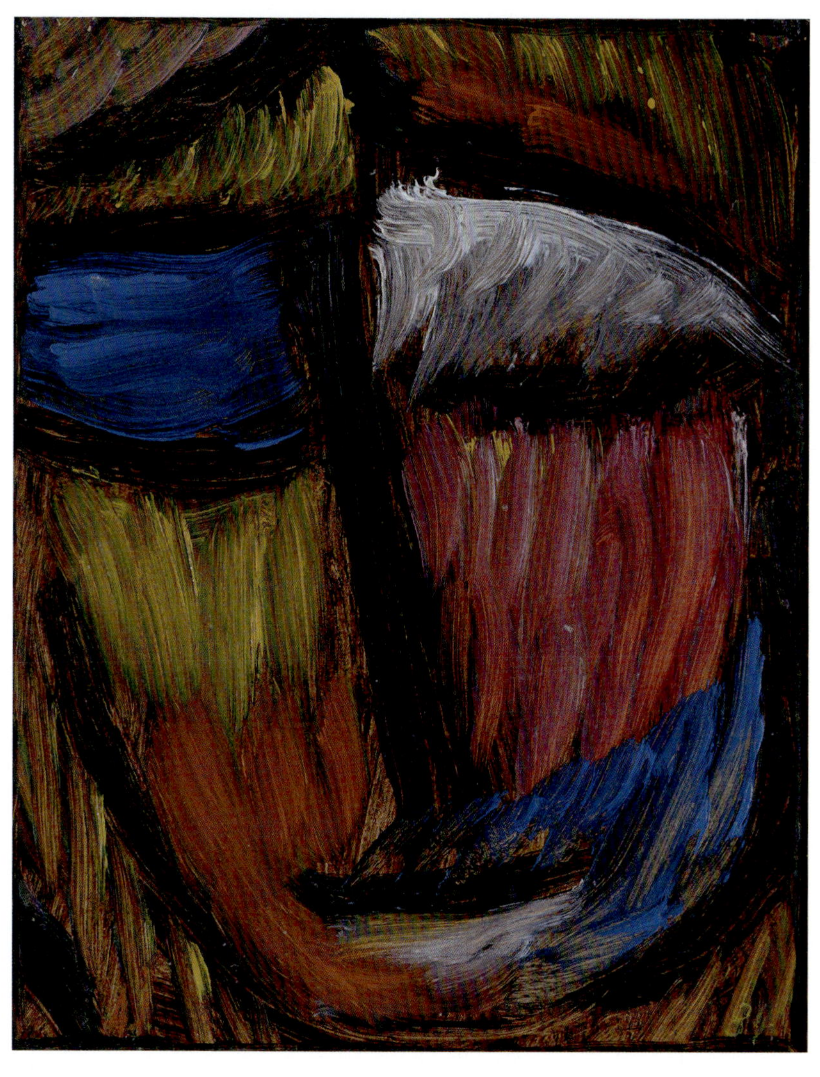

MEDITATION (N. 30), 1934

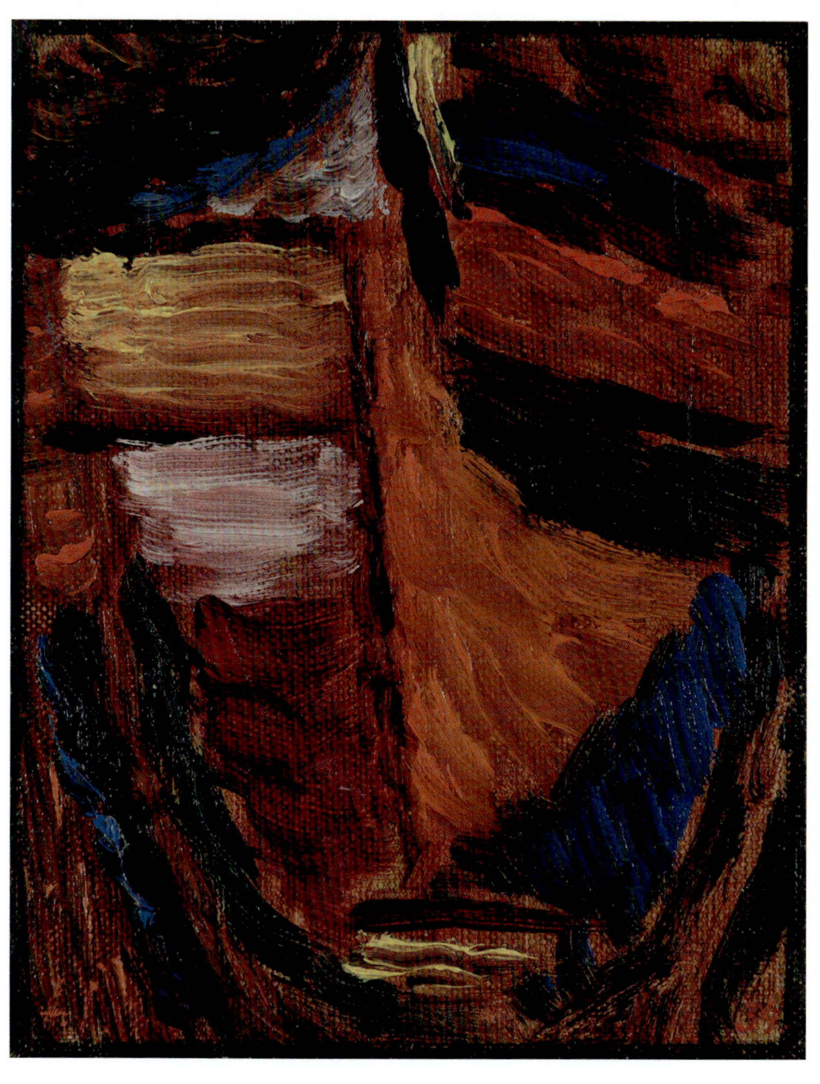

MEDITATION: IN MEMORY OF MY AILING HANDS (N. 5), 1934

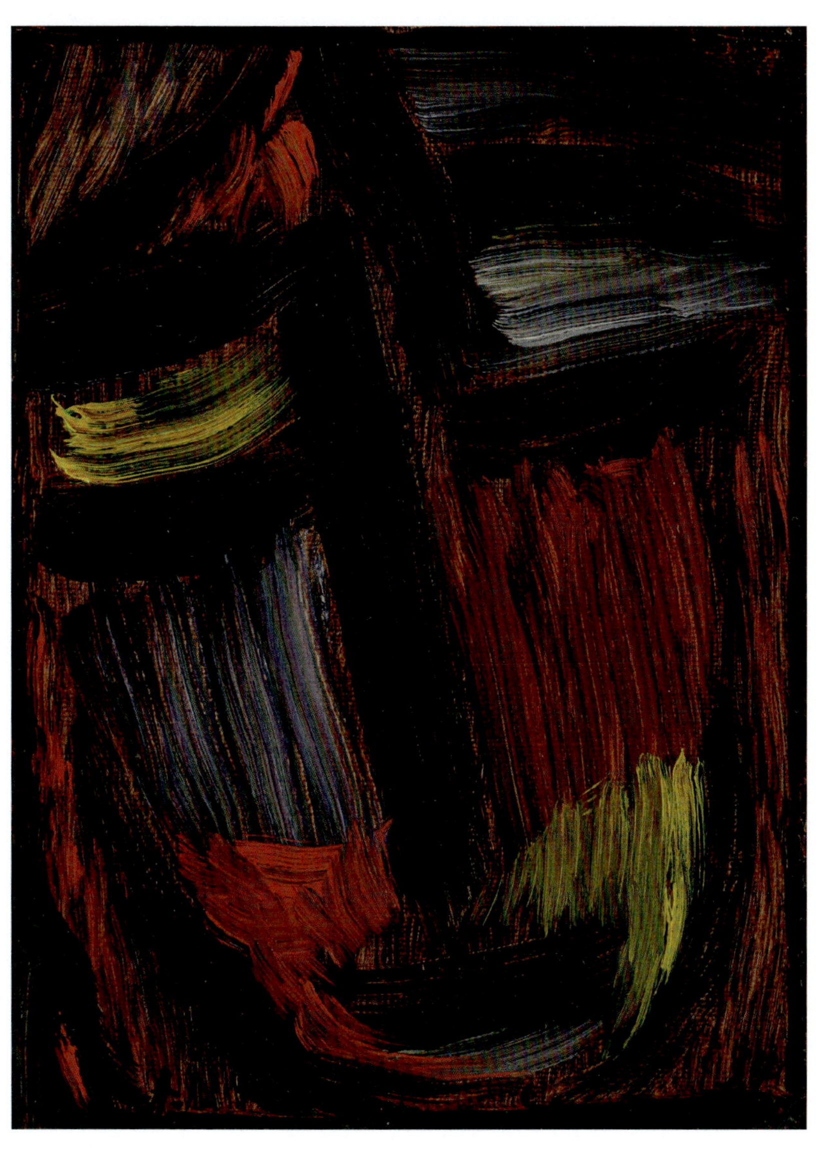

MEDITATION (N. 290), 1934

MEDITATION (N. 57), 1935

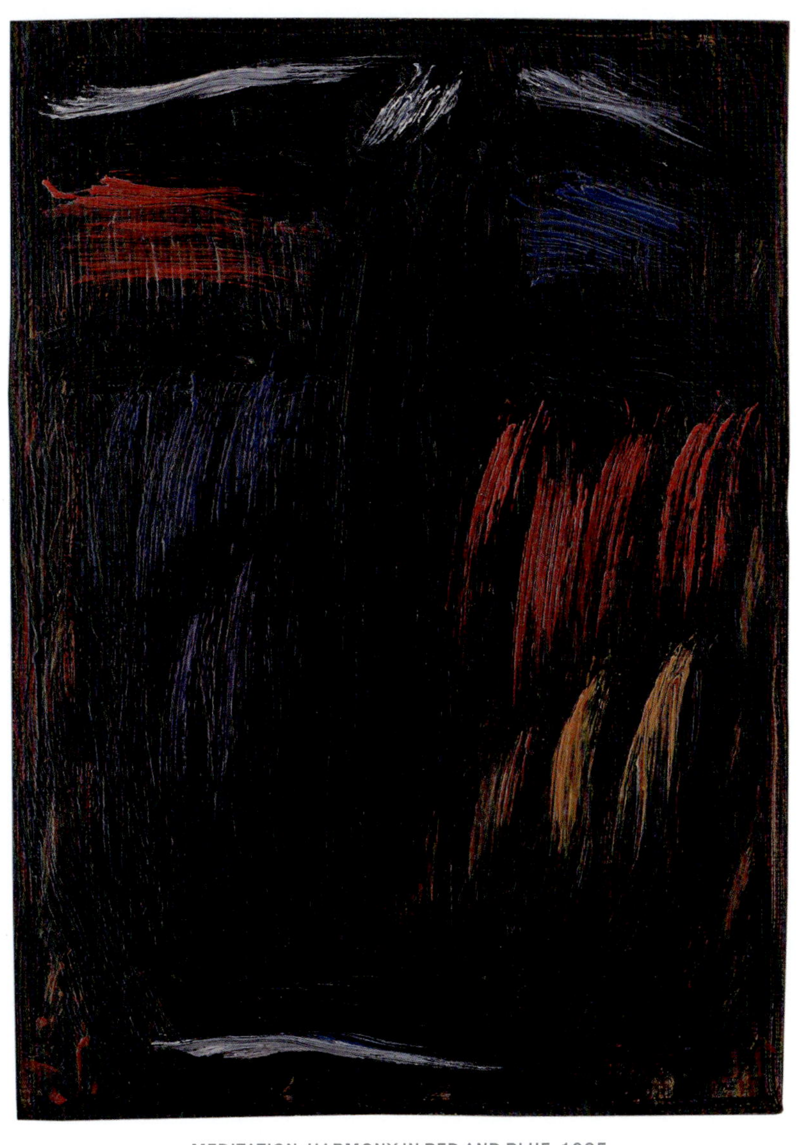

MEDITATION: HARMONY IN RED AND BLUE, 1935

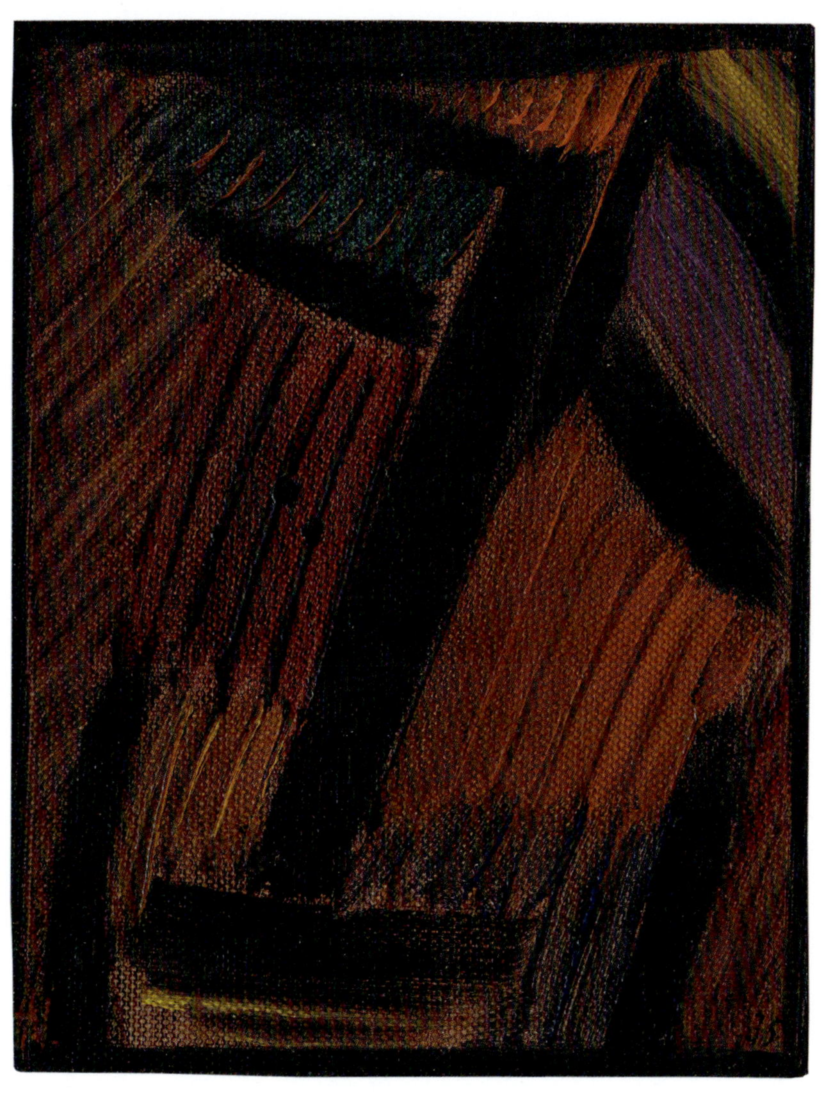

MEDITATION (N. 87), 1935

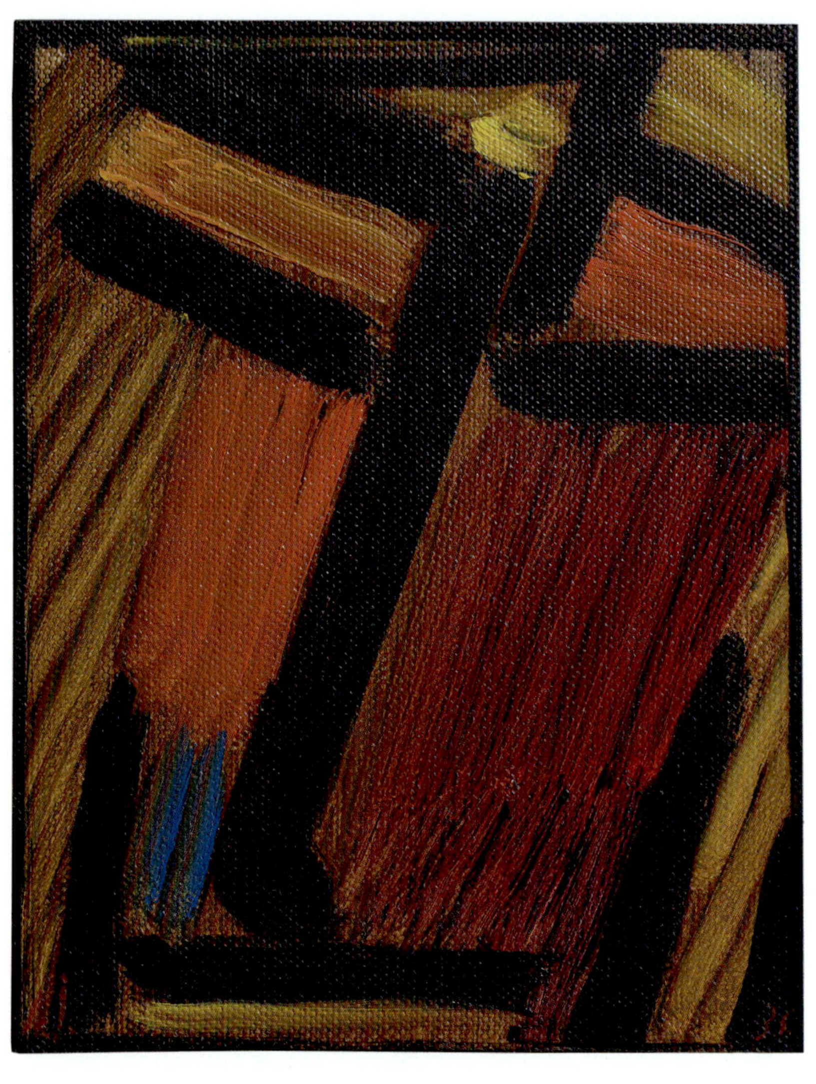

MEDITATION: SMALL HEAD (N. 120), 1935

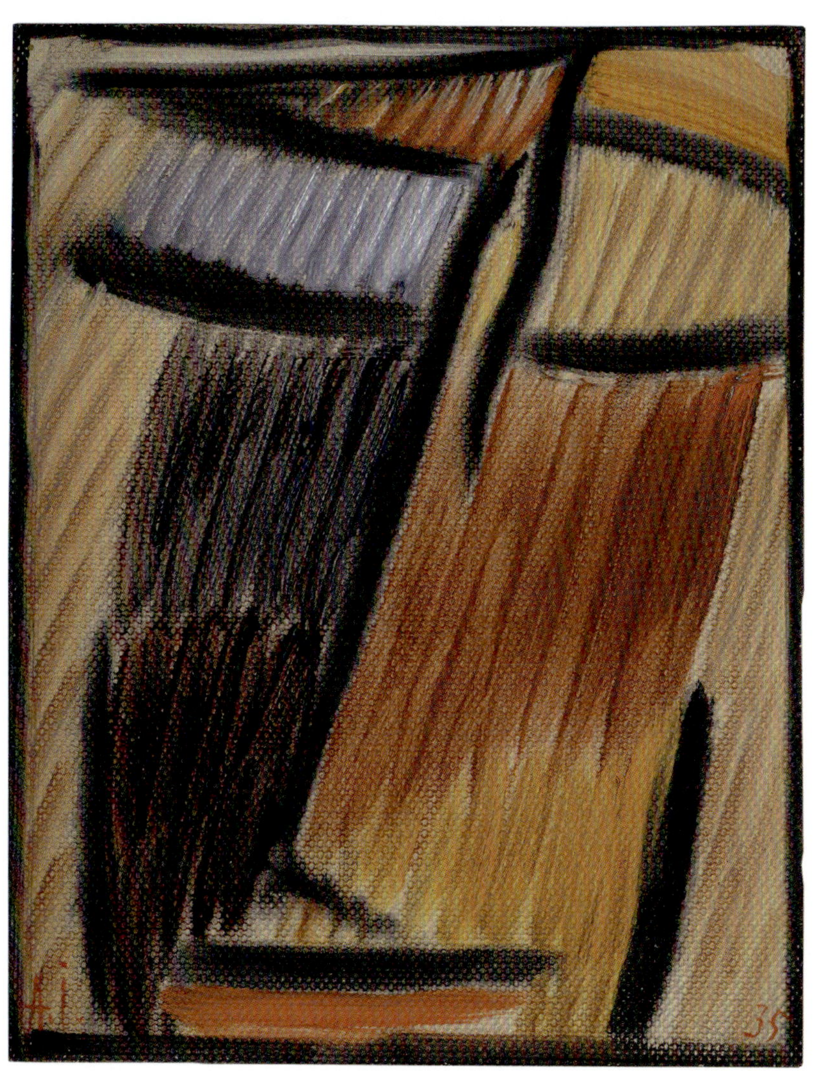

MEDITATION (N. 95), 1935

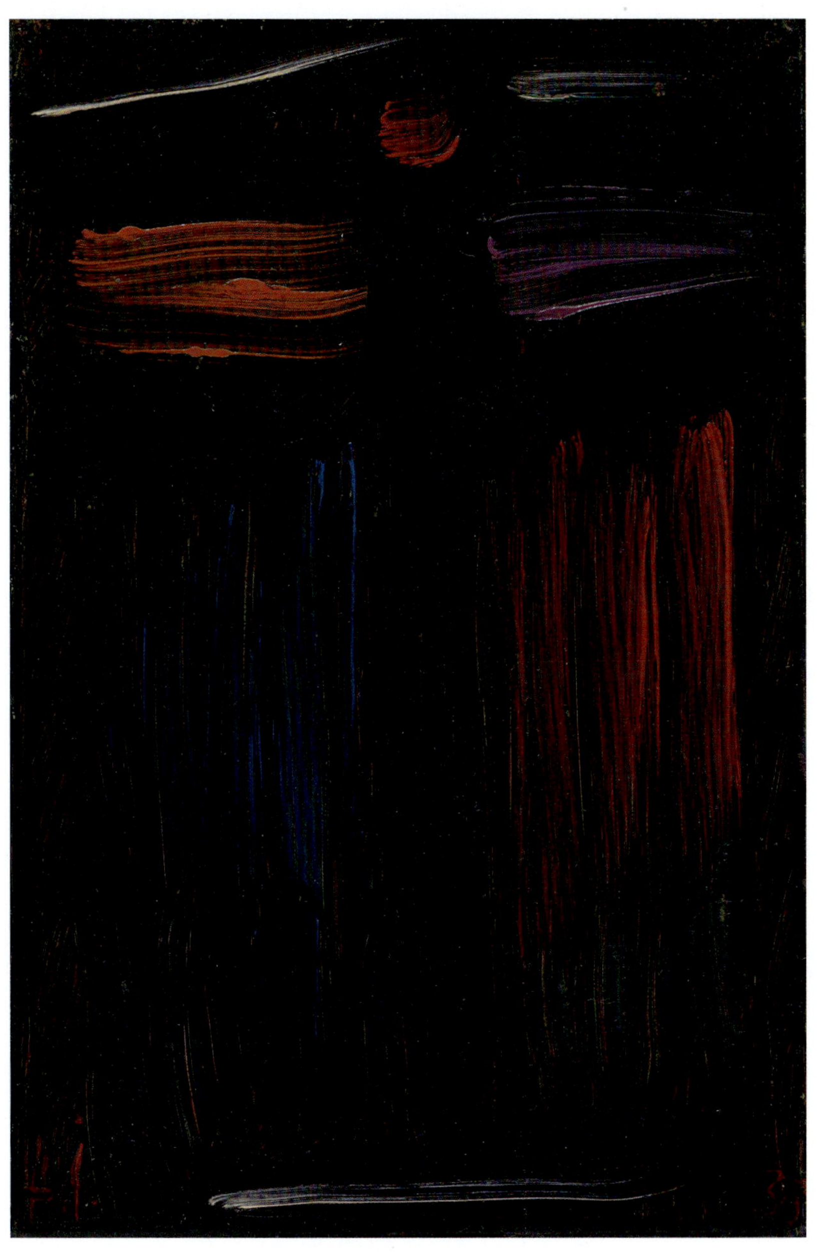

MEDITATION (N. 33), 1935

MEDITATION: LOOKING BACK (II N. 83), 1935

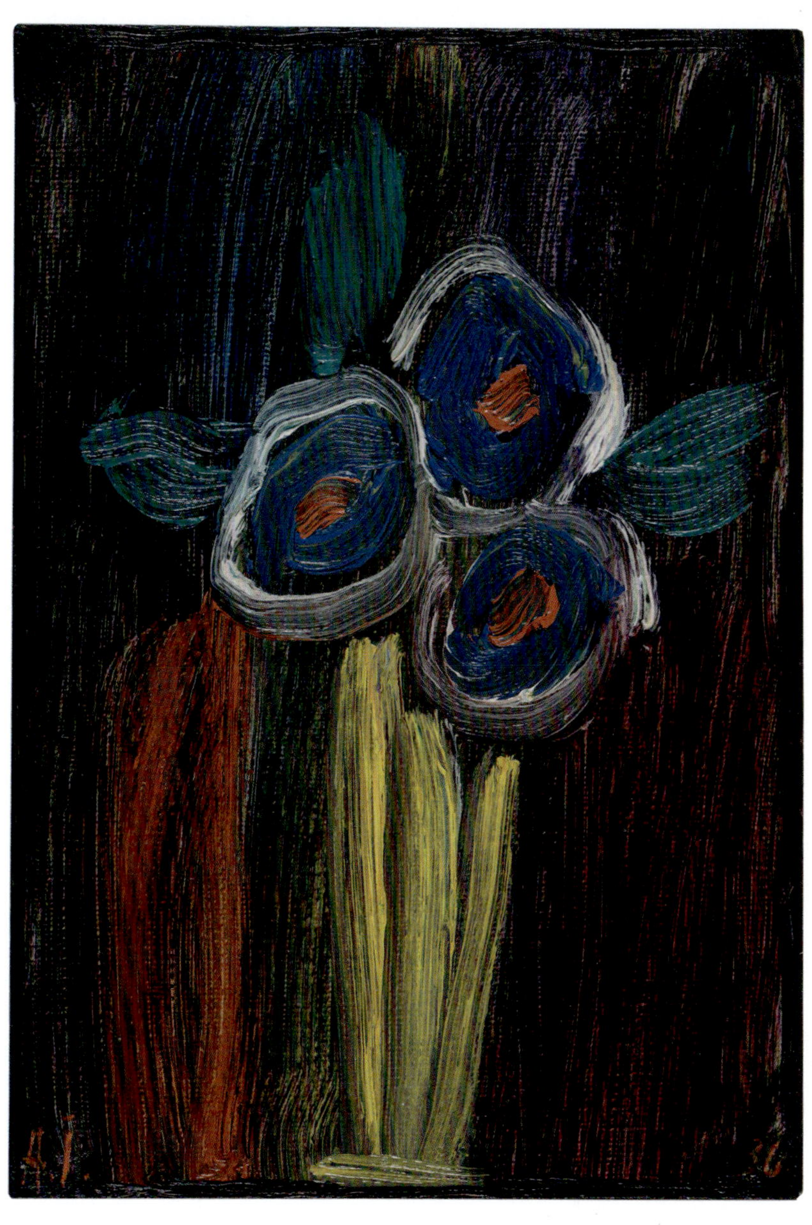

STILL LIFE (YELLOW VASE (III N. 32), 1936

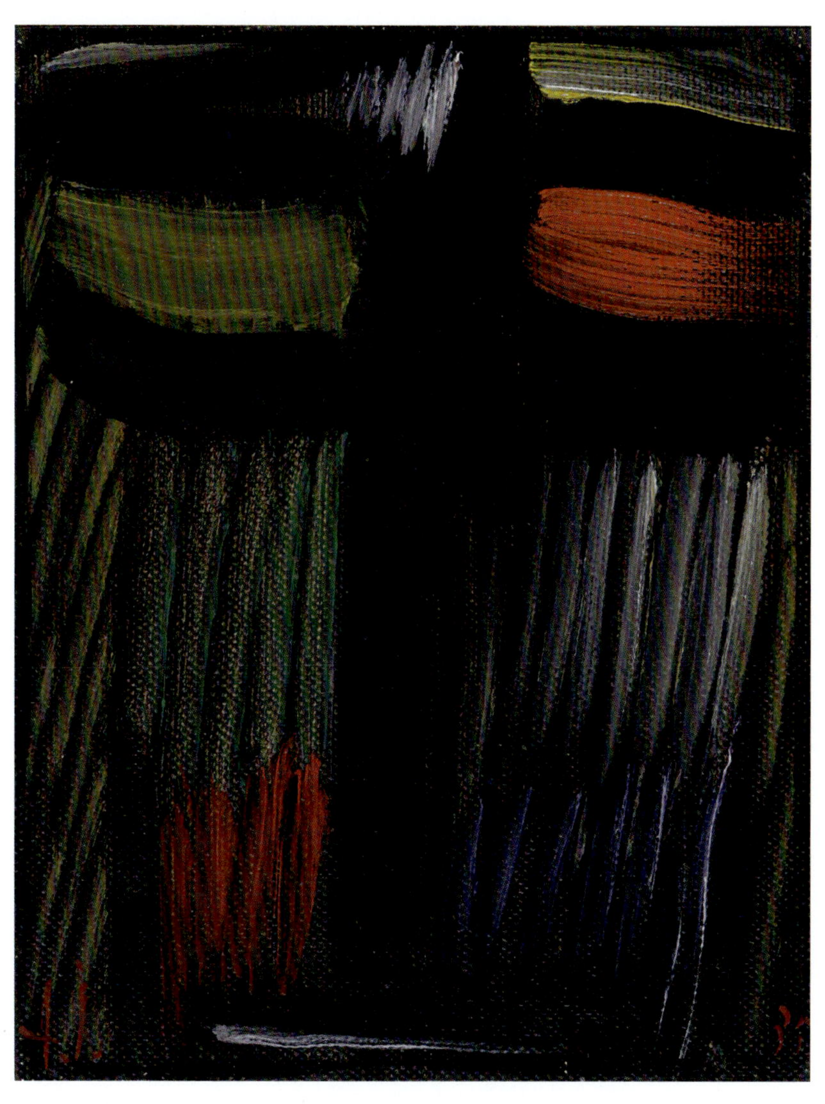

MEDITATION (N. 133), 1935

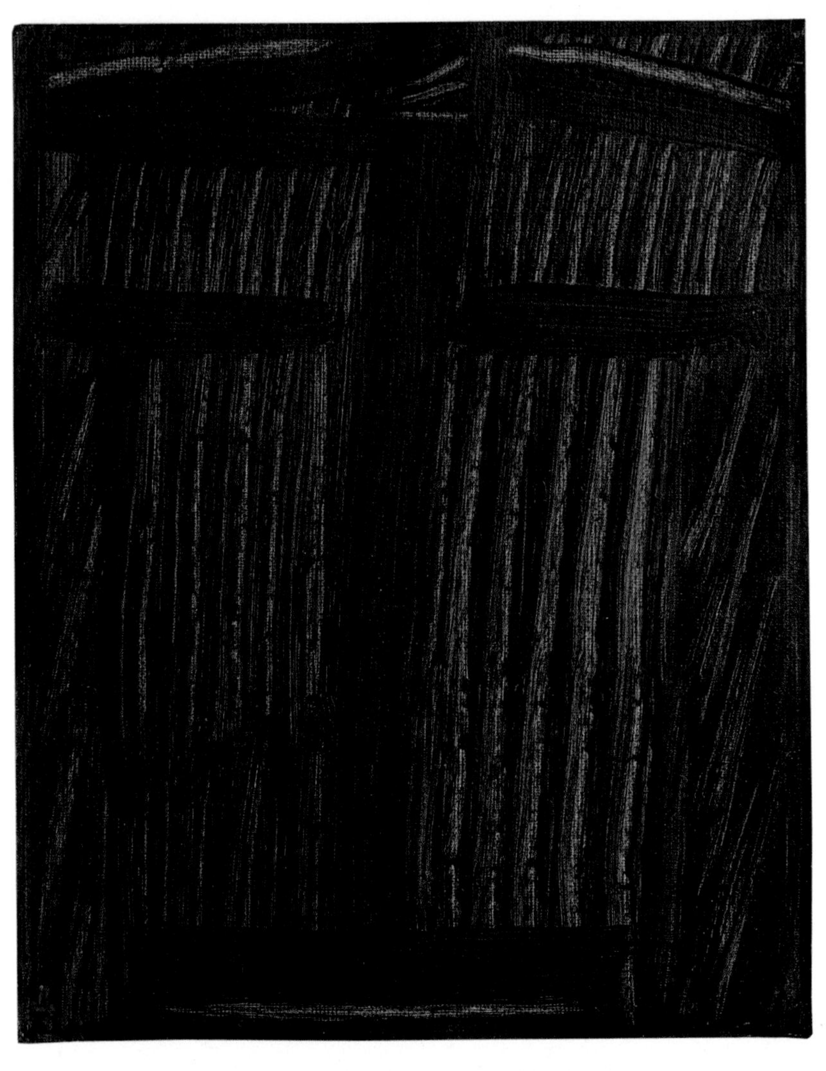

LARGE MEDITATION: IN THE THICKET (N. 24), 1937

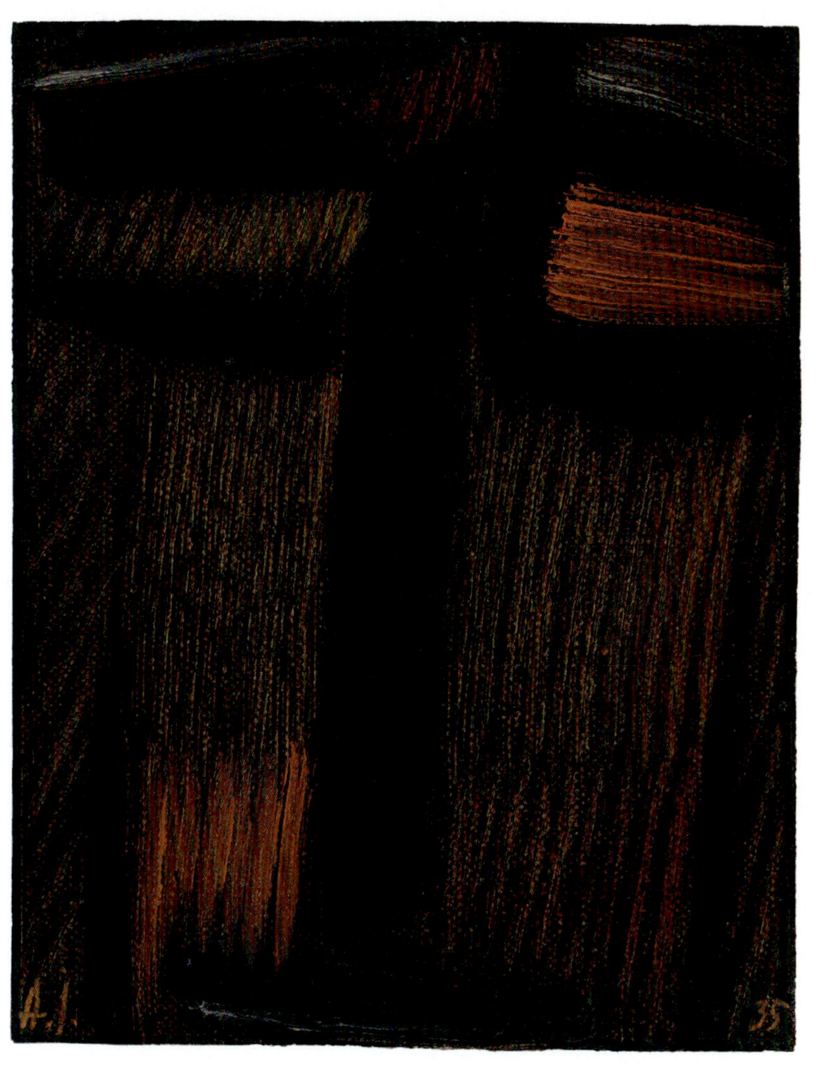

MEDITATION: IT SHINES WITHIN ME, COME TO ME, 1935

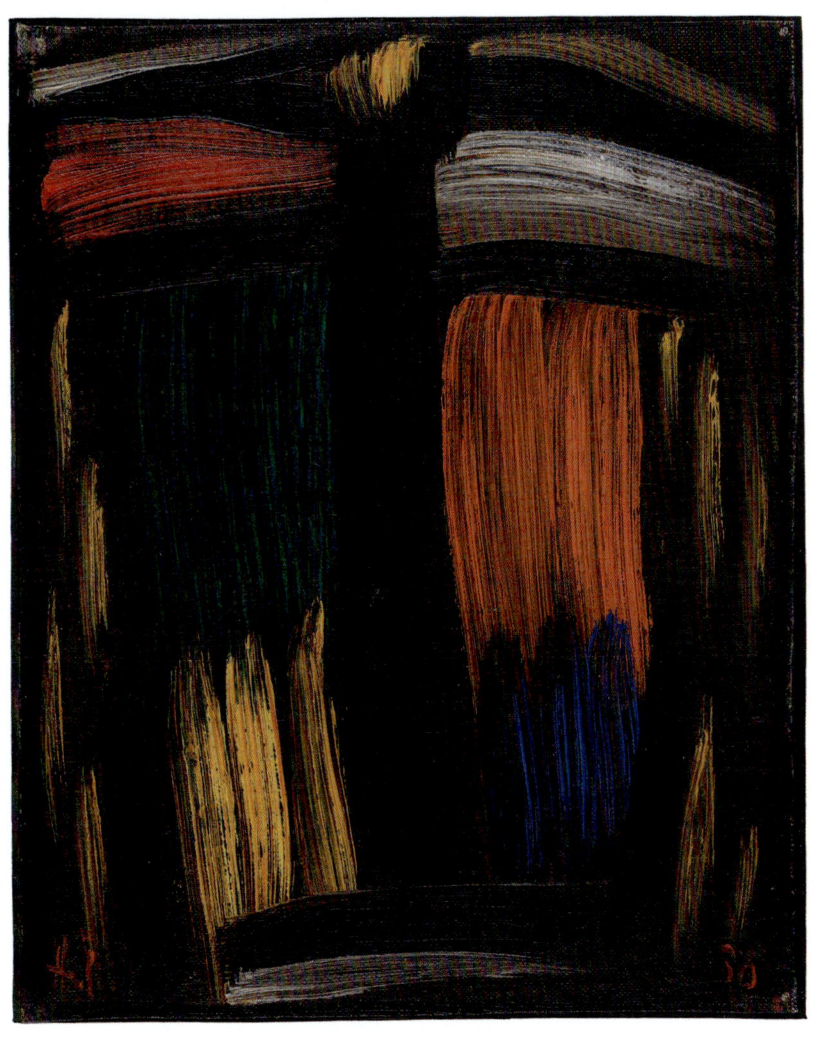

LARGE MEDITATION: GLOW (VI N. 24), 1936

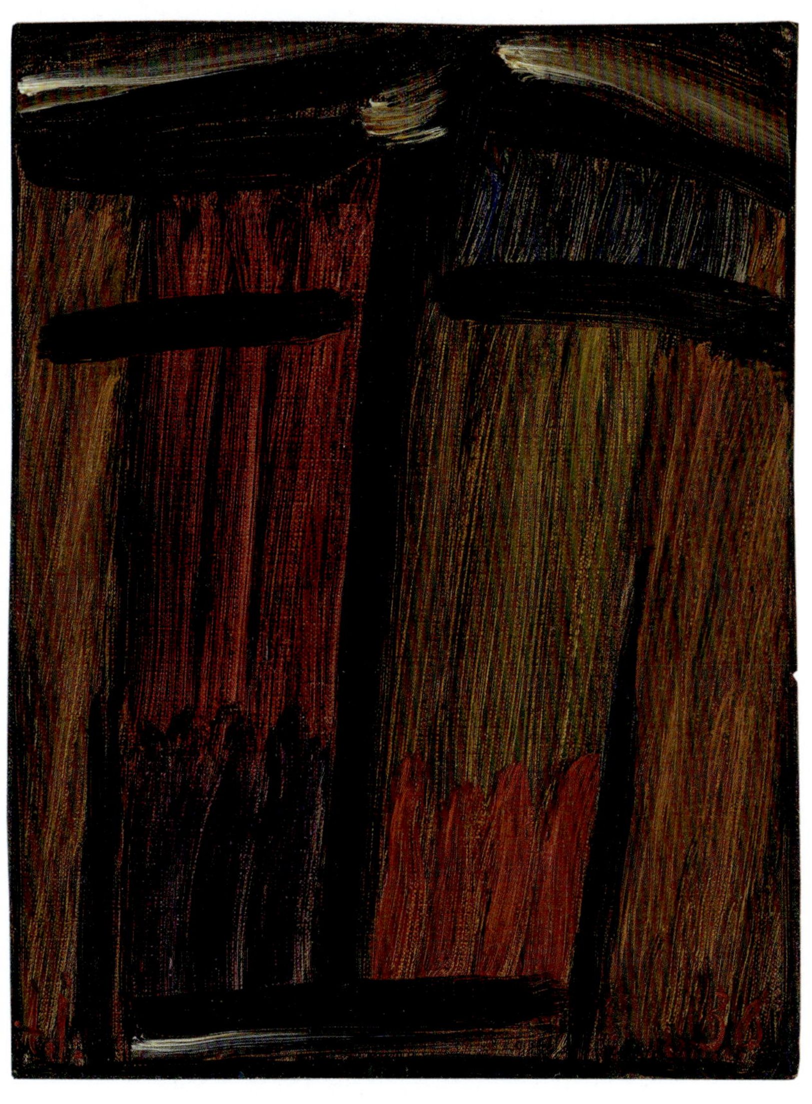

LARGE MEDITATION: MOURNING BECOMES ELECTRA, 1936

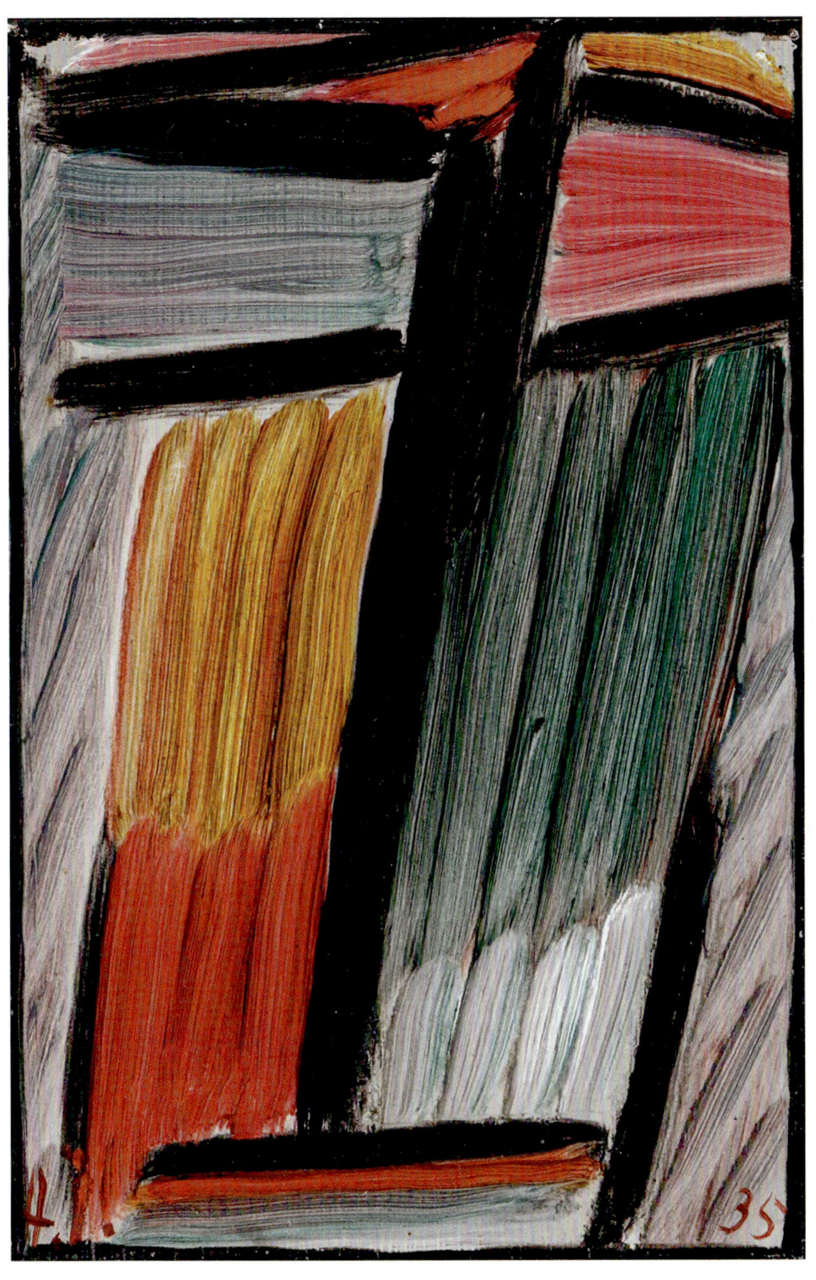

MEDITATION: A RUSHING SOUND APPROACHED, 1935

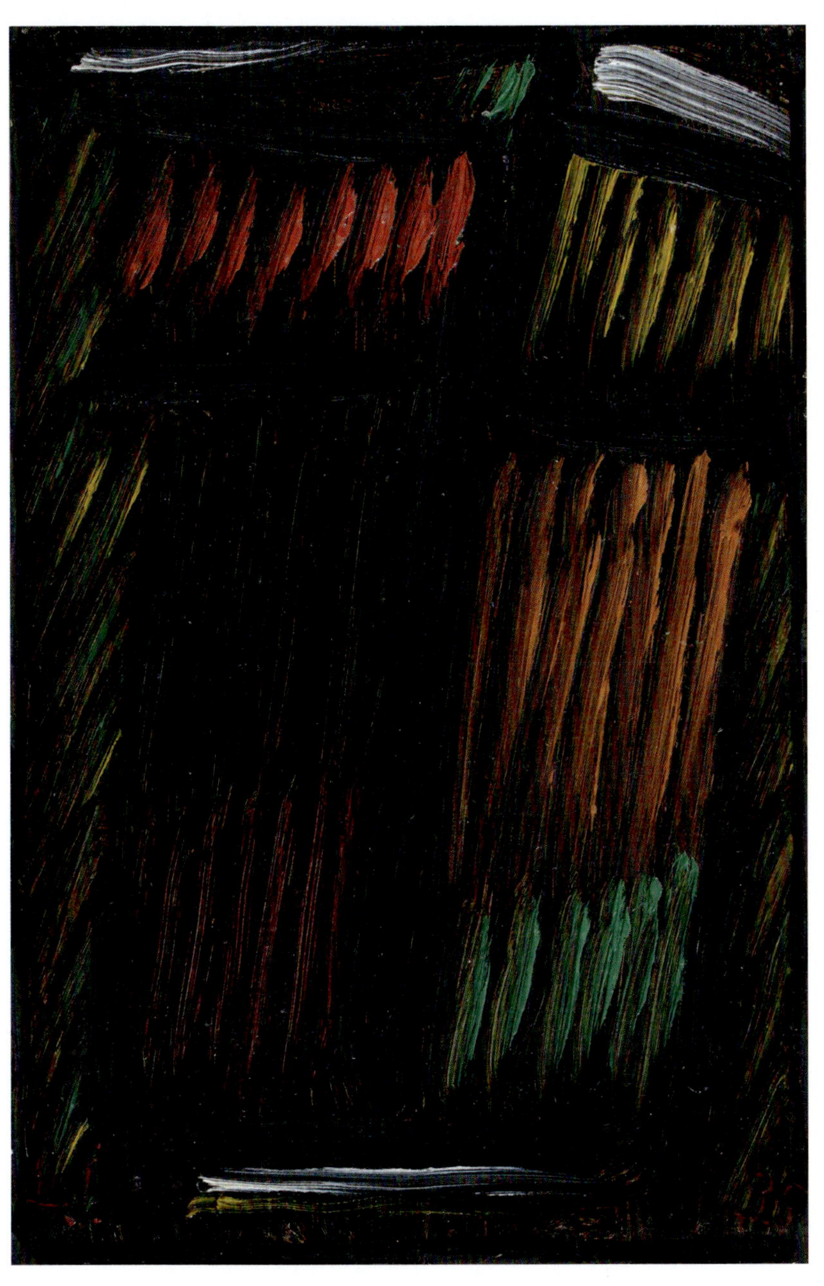

MEDITATION: FORGET ME NOT, 1935

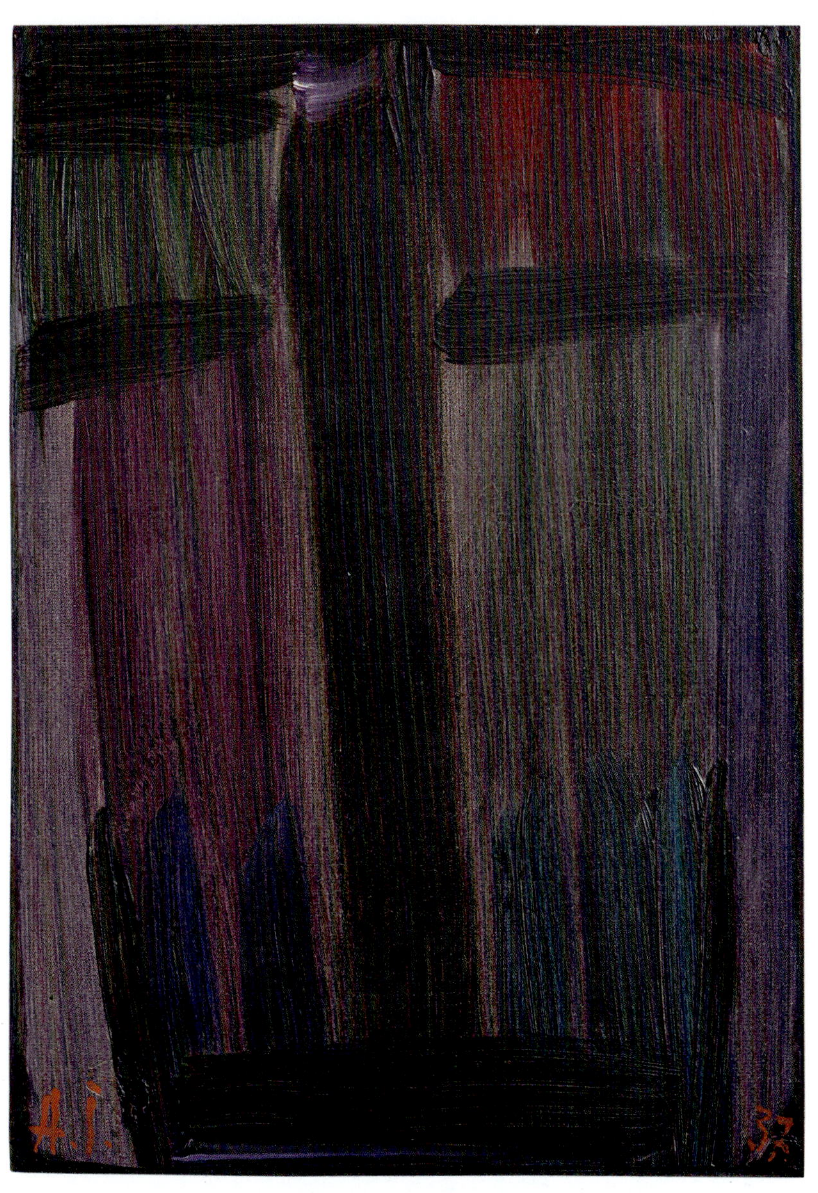

LARGE MEDITATION (N. 6), 1937

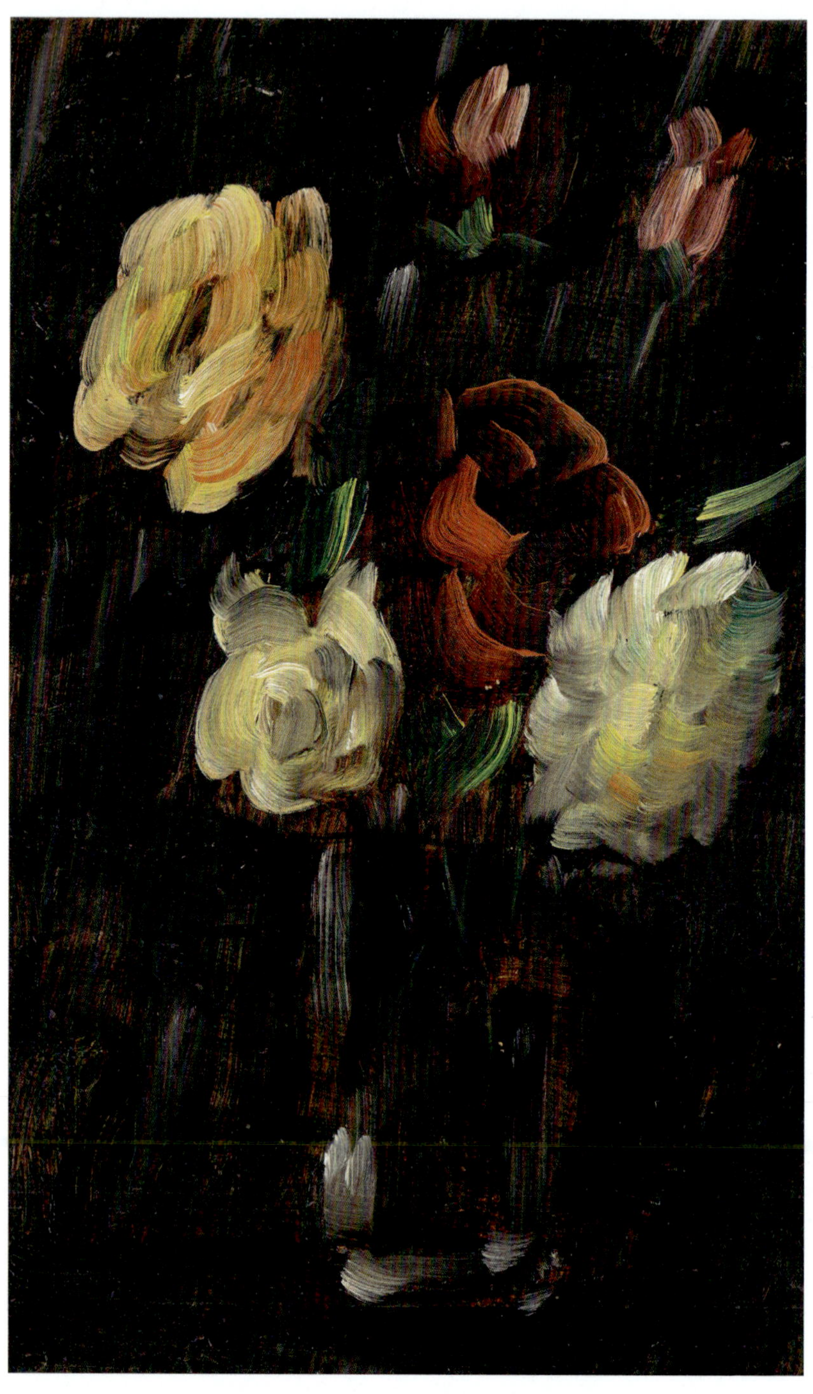

LARGE STILL LIFE: STILL LIFE ON BLACK BACKGROUND,
CLEAR GLASS WITH PINK AND RED ROSES, 1937

ENCYCLOPAEDIA JAWLENSKY

ABSTRACTION

In the early part of the 20th century, many artists were working towards abstraction. Historically, Jawlensky's friend and fellow artist Kandinsky has been credited with inventing abstract painting, but in recent years art historians have pointed to another important precursor, the Swedish artist Hilma af Klint. While Jawlensky had no desire to make completely abstract paintings, he did use the term in the title of his series *Abstract Heads*. In the last two decades of his life, as he focussed on the subject of the face, his art became increasingly non-representational.

ALL-RUSSIAN EXHIBITION

Jawlensky's first encounter with art was at the All-Russian Exhibition of Industry and Art in Moscow in 1882. As Jawlensky writes, he came to "a section devoted to art – there were only paintings, and this was the first time in my life I had seen paintings – I was so deeply affected that it was a case of Saul becoming Paul. It was the turning point of my life. Ever since then art has been my ideal, my holy of holies, that for which my soul and my entire self yearn."

ANDREAS

Andreas Nesnakomoff Jawlensky (1902-1984) was born from a relationship between Jawlensky and Werefkin's maid, Helene, whom he later married. Andreas had inherited his father's talent for painting, and from his early childhood they would often paint together. There is even some question whether certain works are by father or son or both in collaboration. An example is *Still Life with Green Vase* (c. 1911) in this exhibition.

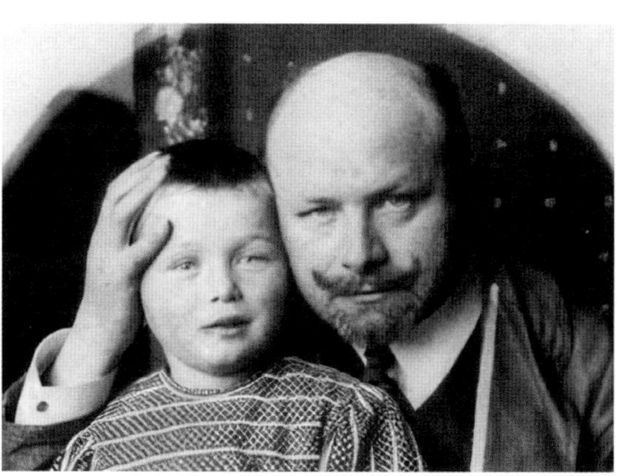

JAWLENSKY WITH HIS SON, ANDREAS, MUNICH 1905

ANDROGYNY

Characteristically, Jawlensky tended not to cultivate stereotypical representations of masculinity and femininity in his paintings. Moreover, Jawlensky often portrayed his close friend, the dancer and choreographer Alexander Sakharoff, in costume, who was known for performing as a woman. Many of Jawlensky's portraits from the years before World War I have a strikingly androgynous nature. With his tight cropping of the subject, zeroing in on the head and neck, we are often left with no clues to tell whether the subject is a man or a woman. *Head of a Youth*, in this catalogue, is an example of this. The tight cropping of the face and the androgynous also became important features of his final two series: his *Abstract Heads* and *Meditations*.

ALEXEJ JAWLENSKY
DANCE STUDY AFTER ALEXANDER SACHAROFF, 1912
PENCIL ON BROWN PAPER, 50 × 33,5 CM

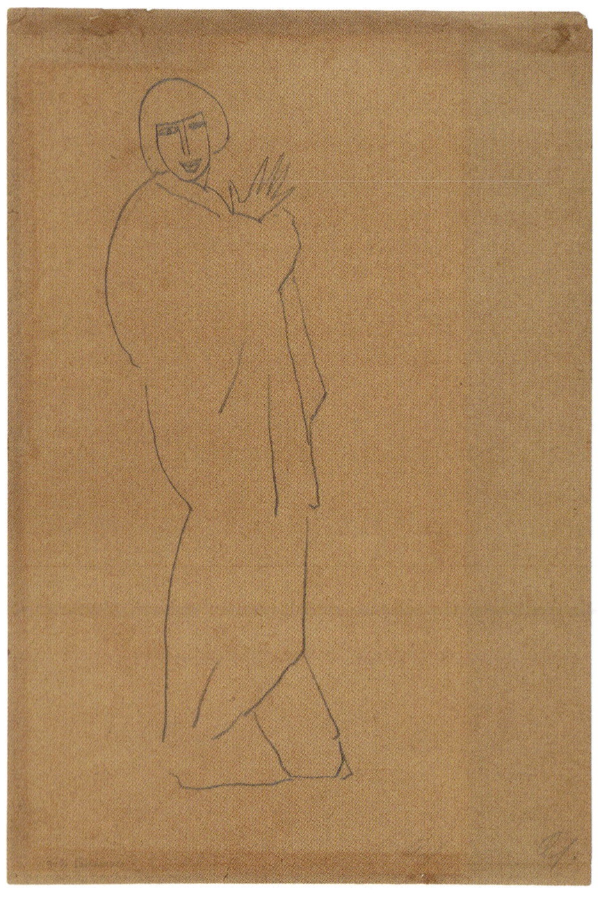

ASCONA

From 1918-1921, during his time in Ascona, Switzerland, Jawlensky began his second-to-last major series, *Abstract Heads*. Ascona was teeming with artists and freethinkers. The writer Rainer Maria Rilke paid a number of visits to Jawlensky and Werefkin. Jawlensky called these years "the most interesting in my life." But his relationship with Werefkin was strained, and they finally went their separate ways after Ascona. Werefkin remained there the rest of her life.

AŽBE

From 1896-1899, Jawlensky and Werefkin attended a famous private painting school in Munich run by the Slovenian painter Anton Ažbe (1862-1905). While Ažbe painted in a relatively conventional style of realism, his teachings attracted many painters who later became famous. Ažbe stressed artistic freedom and encouraged his students to paint with pure colours. As Jawlensky later wrote, during their time with Ažbe they learned new things about drawing and form. Kandinsky arrived at the school while Jawlensky and Werefkin were there, and they introduced him to Munich's avant-garde art scene.

BALTIC EXHIBITION

In the summer of 1914, a historic event took place in Malmö, Sweden. Around 850,000 people visited an exhibition of some 3,500 works by artists from Denmark, Sweden, Russia and Germany. Jawlensky organised the Russian contribution to the exhibition, which included works by himself and, among others, Kandinsky, Werefkin and Ilya Repin and Werefkin. A notable Swedish contributor was Hilma af Klint, though works by women artists were less prominently displayed than the men's. The exhibition was cut short by the outbreak of World War I on 28 July 1914.

BAUHAUS

Walter Gropius, founder of Bauhaus, invited Jawlensky to teach at the school in the 1920s, which Jawlensky's close friends and collaborators, Kandinsky and Klee, were connected to. However, Jawlensky declined, because he did not feel that art could be taught. He did visit the school in Weimar and contributed to a print portfolio published by Bauhaus in 1921. This print was part of his, at that point, brand new series, *Abstract Heads*, which has strong links to Bauhaus aesthetics.

BIRTH

Jawlensky was born on 25 March 1864 in Torzhok in the Russian province of Tver.

DER BLAUE REITER

In December 1911, after a painting by Kandinsky was rejected by NKVM's selection committee, Kandinsky, Münter and Franz Marc left the association. Soon after, they formed the Blaue Reiter group and organised an exhibition featuring their own works alongside those of artists like Robert Delaunay (Jawlensky bought one of his exhibited works), Paul Klee, August Macke and the Austrian composer Arnold Schönberg. In May of the following year, they published *Der Blaue Reiter Almanak*, mixing images and texts by and about Blaue Reiter artists with Bavarian folklore, African masks, role models from art history and much more. While Jawlensky was not officially a member of the group, he is often described as such, and certainly shared many of the same influences and exhibited with the members.

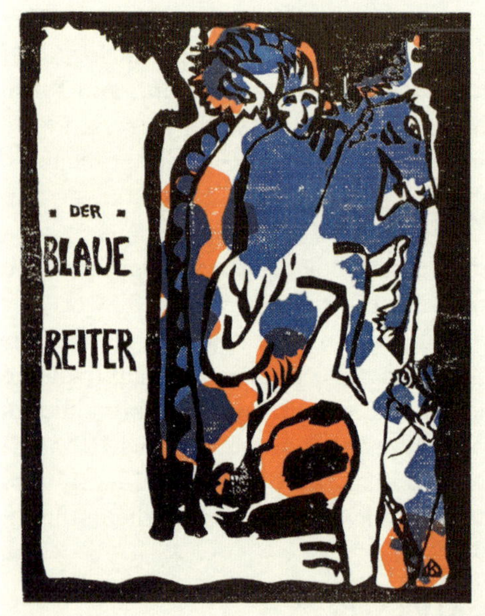

TITLE PAGE BY WASSILY KANDINSKY FOR *THE BLUE RIDER* (DER BLAUE REITER) *ALMANAC*, 1912

THE BLUE FOUR

Der Blaue Reiter was an avant-garde group, while the Blue Four was a more practical partnership between Kandinsky, Klee, Lyonel Feininger and Jawlensky. The name echoes Der Blaue Reiter, highlighting blue as a spiritual colour for the four artists. Jawlensky's close friend and agent, Emmy "Galka" Scheyer, took the initiative to form the group. Promoting the artists in Europe and the United States, Scheyer played a key role in bridging European and American art. Exhibitions of the Blue Four acquainted American artists, including big names like Arshile Gorky and Robert Motherwell, with European modernism.

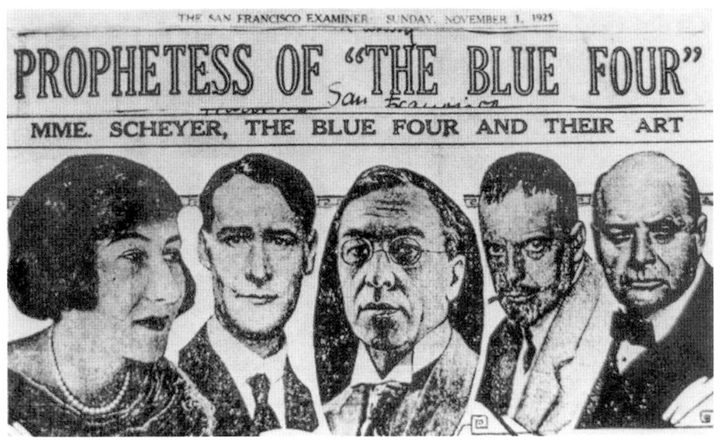

CAGE

In 1935, the American artist and composer John Cage (1912-1992) bought a *Meditation* for 25 dollars in instalments. In broken German, he wrote the artist, "Mr Jawlensky, I can't write German or speak it, but I'm overjoyed because I've bought one of your pictures: Now it is in me. I write music. You are my teacher." In 1939, Cage organised an exhibition with the Blue Four in Seattle, buying two more paintings by Jawlensky. As Cage's library reveals, late in life, in 1987, he received a Jawlensky catalogue from a New York gallery. Apparently, Cage remained fascinated by Jawlensky throughout his life. Cage's strong ties to major painters like Mark Rothko and Jasper Johns increases the likelihood that they were intimately familiar with Jawlensky's late works.

COLOUR

Among his fellow artists, Jawlensky was known as a brilliant colourist. His use of colour was profoundly inspired by Van Gogh and Gauguin, as well as by Matisse and the other Fauvists who experimented with a non-naturalistic palette. In his studio on Giselastrasse in Munich, his partner, Werefkin, had even set up a colour laboratory. Once Jawlensky began working with repeating motifs, the form of the works was given in advance, freeing him to make endless experiments with colour effects. His late *Meditations* are painted on a dark background in different combinations of colours from one painting to the next – orange against blue, orange against green. The colours of his final works are delicately muted to the point of resembling coloured embers in the dark.

DEATH

After years of illness, Jawlensky died on 15 March 1941 in Wiesbaden and is buried in the Russian Orthodox church cemetery there. In his memoirs from 1937, he describes his last paintings, the *Meditations*, as an artistic last will and testament: "And now I leave these small but, to me, important works to the future and to people who love art."

DEGENERATE ART

In 1933, the National Socialists banned Jawlensky from exhibiting in Germany. A number of his works were confiscated, and many have since been lost. That year, his works were included in *Kulturbolschewistische Bilder* at Kunsthalle Mannheim, a precursor to the infamous *Entartete Kunst* exhibition of "degenerate art" held in 1937 at Hofgartenarkaden in Munich and elsewhere. *Entartete Kunst* included two paintings and several works on paper by Jawlensky, and the artist visited the exhibition in a wheelchair with a friend. It was his last trip out of Wiesbaden. Jawlensky could not understand the Nazi position on his art, writing "I am not allowed to exhibit my works here. Why not? My art is not in any way subversive. And I am not a Bolshevik, neither in my art nor in my life. My art is nothing more than meditation, or prayer in colour. And it is not possible for it to harm anyone."

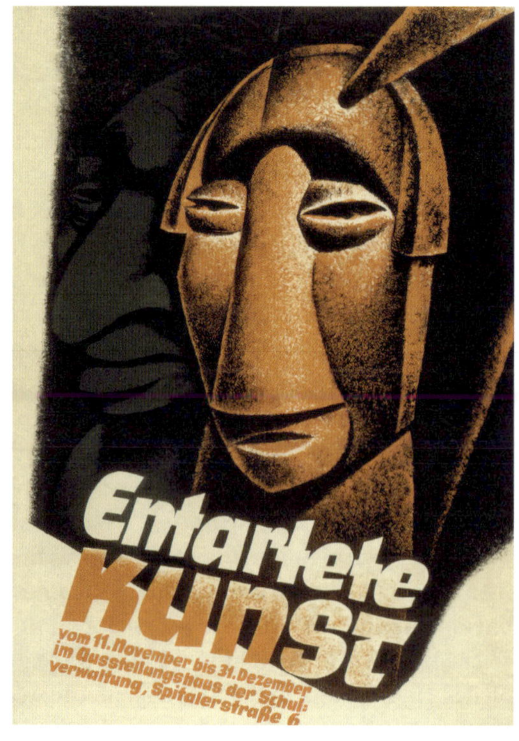

POSTER FOR THE EXHIBITION
ENTARTETE KUNST
(DEGENERATE ART), 1937

DELAUNAY (ROBERT AND SONIA)

Robert Delaunay (1885-1941) was among the French artists who captivated the German Expressionists. His work was not least featured in the groundbreaking *Blaue Reiter Almanak* and was the subject of an essay in the publication. In 1906, Jawlensky met the Russian artist Sonia Terk, the future Sonia Delaunay (1885-1979), at the *L'art russe* exhibition in Paris. In 1911, in connection with the first Blaue Reiter exhibition, he acquired a painting by Robert Delaunay, *La Ville* (1910). He sold the painting in 1925 when he was short of money, and it has since been lost. Like Jawlensky, Robert Delaunay often worked in series with minor compositional variations but great variety of colour. Delaunay's series *Les Fenêtres* (1912-13) were surely a big inspiration for Jawlensky's *Variations*.

ERSTER DEUTSCHER HERBSTSALON

In September 1913, a watershed exhibition opened at Herwarth Walden's Berlin gallery Der Sturm. The *Erster Deutscher Herbstsalon* presented the latest developments in European art, and many of the participants are still considered leading artists of the period. They included Kandinsky, Hans Arp, Natalia Goncharova, Piet Mondrian, Jawlensky and Werefkin, alongside three important artists that the Louisiana has showcased in recent years – Marsden Hartley, Sonia Delaunay and Münter.

EXOTICISM

Historically referred to as "exotic" and "primitive," non-Western art and craft was collected in Europe and exhibited in museums in cities like Paris, Berlin and Munich and in private collections, where they attracted scores of artists. While we don't know whether Jawlensky was among them, he did create a portrait series of women from around the world, and his *Abstract Heads* have obvious mask-like features. The title of one 1933 work even refers to Africa (*Abstract Head (Africa)*), while *Exotic Head* (1917) shows a non-Western figure that the artist might have seen.

EXPRESSIONISM

Jawlensky is generally classified as an Expressionist. Expressionism embraces different artistic styles often characterised by bold colours and vigorous, expressive brushwork. It is concerned with communicating an internal experience of the external world. The earliest Expressionist movement in Germany arose with the artist group Die Brücke in Dresden in 1905. Members included Ernst Ludwig Kirchner and Karl Schmitt Rotluff, as well as Jawlensky's friends Cuno Amiet and Nolde. Several of Jawlensky's early portraits show the influence of

Die Brücke in the depiction of the human figure. One notable example is *Head of a Youth*, in this exhibition.

FACES

During the last two decades of his career, Jawlensky mainly painted faces, which gradually became more stylised and eventually with closed eyes. The face became the central motif for Jawlensky because it best expressed his spirituality. A conclusion he came to not least because of his interest in the Russian icons he grew up looking at. "I found it necessary to find a form for the face, because I had come to understand that great art can only be painted with religious feeling. And that I could only bring to the human face."

GAUGUIN

The French painter Paul Gauguin (1848-1903) was a role model for many young artists at the turn of the 20th century, not least the German Expressionists of Der Blaue Reiter. His paintings of Tahiti, celebrating the island's culture, prefigured the younger generation's interest in the 'exotic' other. In Munich, Jawlensky befriended Felix vom Rath, a young, very wealthy composer. It was at Vom Rath's home that Jawlensky first saw a painting by Gauguin, *Riders on the Beach in Tahiti* (1902). In his 1937 memoirs, Jawlensky recalled this encounter as a turning point in his artistic development. He also saw a major Gauguin retrospective at the Grand Palais in Paris in 1906, while he was exhibiting in *L'art russe* at the same location.

PAUL GAUGUIN, *RIDERS ON THE BEACH IN TAHITI*, 1902
PRIVATE COLLECTION

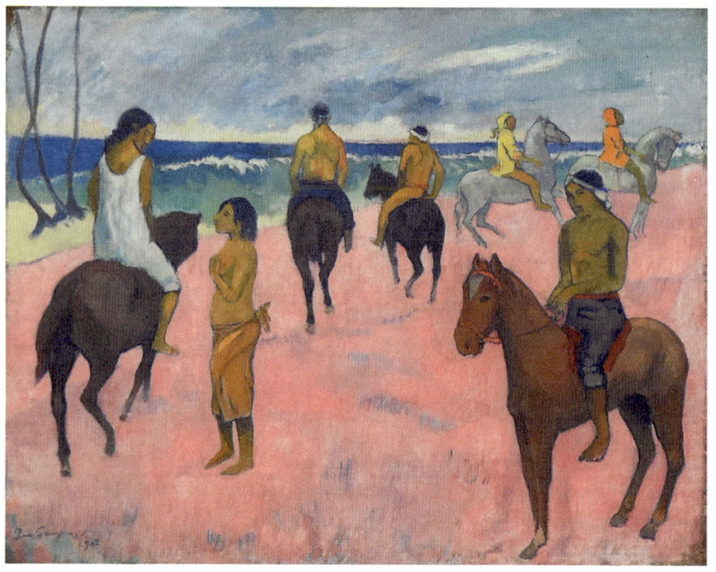

HELENE NESNAKOMOFF

Helene Nesnakomoff (1881-1965) was Werefkin's maid and moved with the couple to Munich in 1896. In 1902, she gave birth to a son, Andreas, fathered by Jawlensky. Theirs was an unconventional arrangement. Jawlensky and Helene were probably more of a romantic couple than he and Werefkin, but Helene didn't sit at the table when they had guests. In 1921, Jawlensky broke definitively with Werefkin, on whom he was financially dependent, and married Helene in 1922.

JAWLENSKY, HELENE NESNAKOMOFF AND ANDREAS
NESNAKOMOFF JAWLENSKY, MUNICH 1919

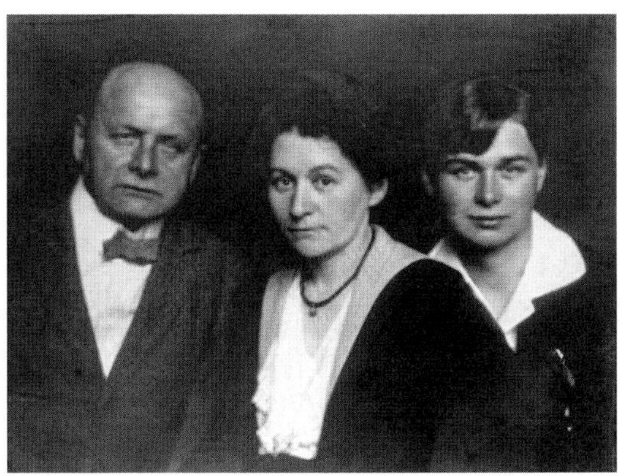

HERMITAGE

During his studies in St. Petersburg in the early 1890s, Jawlensky would often visit the Hermitage Museum with its exceptional collections of Russian icons and Rembrandts. In his memoirs, he wrote of Rembrandt, "Although at the time I understood little of his secret mysticism, his magical art attracted me deeply. I felt closer to the art of Repin, however, because of its vitality and colourfulness. Today, after all these years I see how ridiculous my judgment was then and I realize the tremendous value of Rembrandt's art."

ICONS

In his memoirs, Jawlensky describes the profound impression made on him by his encounter with the famous *Black Madonna* icon in a church in Częstochowa, Poland. Icons were an ideal for Jawlensky's artistic project, as they were for other artists at the time, including Kasimir Malevich and Matisse. Jawlensky's paintings of faces are stylised in a similar way to Russian icons. He saw the faces as representing something greater – the whole universe. He even painted some of his late *Meditations* on gold leaf to underscore their icon-like qualities and likened them to "biblical heads".

ILLNESS

Jawlensky began to suffer from rheumatoid arthritis in the late 1920s, and it grew progressively worse. Eventually, his illness made him unable to paint like before. Out of raw necessity, he came up with a technique that allowed him to paint simplified subjects by gripping the brush with both hands. In fact, this limitation provided a creative breakthrough, as he discovered the imperative that gave rise to the *Meditations*. In a letter he wrote, "I have no external experiences, and that is why I only paint what is in my soul, what lies deep within me, like a meditation focussed inward, and my language is colour. The paintings are mostly dark. The colours are so mysterious, so deep." By early 1938, Jawlensky was no longer able to paint.

JAWLENSKY IN HIS BED WITH HIS OWN WORKS ON THE WALL, C. 1940

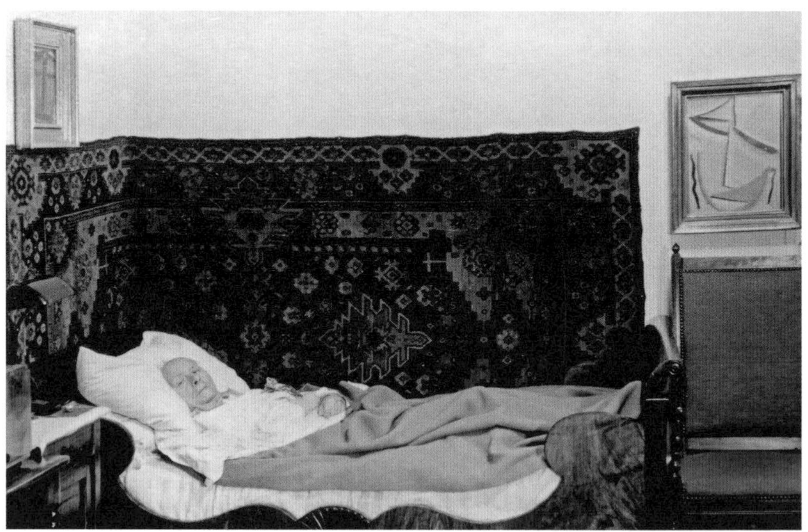

KANDINSKY

Jawlensky and Wassily Kandinsky (1866-1944) met in the late 1890s at Anton Ažbe's painting school in Munich. The meeting was pivotal to both artists, who periodically worked closely together despite their very different approaches to painting. Clearly, Kandinsky had a major impact on Jawlensky's work – both through his involvement in NKVM and Der Blaue Reiter, and through his writings about art, especially *Concerning the Spiritual in Art*, which highlighted the connection between painting and music. Conversely, Jawlensky and Werefkin were instrumental in Kandinsky's career by introducing him to the Southern German avant-garde.

KLEE

The artist Paul Klee (1879-1940) was a lifelong friend of Jawlensky. He traded more works with him than with any other artist. The two met through Kandinsky, and Klee showed in *The First Exhibition of the Editorial Board of The Blue Rider*. Moreover, Klee and Jawlensky were both members of the Blue Four group that influenced the American art scene.

LANDSCAPES AND STILL LIFES

Jawlensky is mainly known for his portraits and faces. However, he also painted numerous landscapes and still lifes. Late in life, when he was severely ill, he made the most of the limited opportunities his arthritic hands permitted to paint vases of flowers. Early on, he worked in landscape, especially during his summers in Murnau and Prerow. His last landscapes, the *Variations*, were based on the view from his window in Saint-Prex and quickly took on a life of their own. When Jawlensky abandoned the *Variations* in 1921, landscape disappeared from his work.

LATE BLOOMER

Jawlensky achieved success in painting relatively late in life. The works in this catalogue and exhibition are all painted by a mature artist. The earliest work, *Murnau Village*, was painted in 1908, when Jawlensky was 44. At that point, Jawlensky had been painting for more than 20 years. He was 50 when he embarked on his singular project of repeating motifs, and 70 when he painted his most distinctive works, the *Meditations*.

WEREFKIN AND JAWLENSKY IN 1893 IN THE STUDIO AT THE BLAGODAT
ESTATE IN WHAT WAS THEN RUSSIAN LITHUANIA

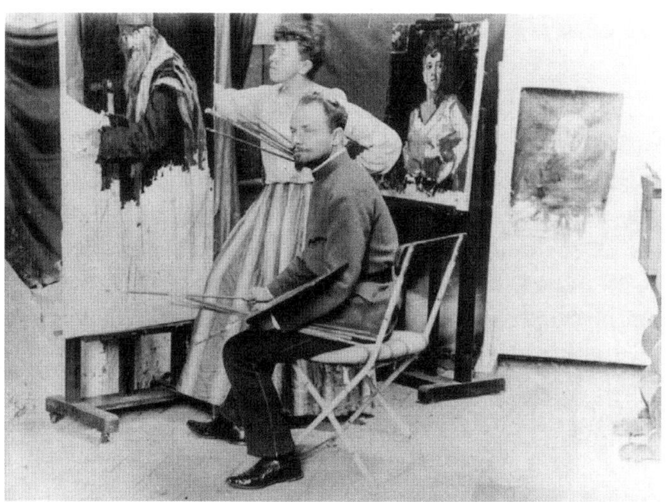

MATISSE

Jawlensky first met Henri Matisse (1869-1954) in 1905 when they were both showing at the Salon d'Automne in Paris. The French artist's style and use of colour, and the work of the Fauvists in general, had an immense impact on Jawlensky, evident not least in his many portraits. Two years later, in 1907, Jawlensky painted in Matisses studio during the summer, and the two met again in 1911.

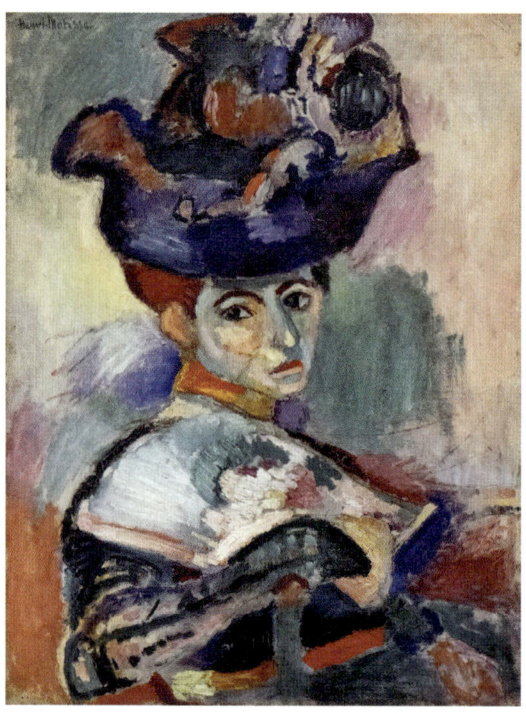

MEDITATIONS

Over roughly four years, from 1934 to 1938, Jawlensky painted his last and by far largest body of work, *Meditations*, comprising some 1,000 pictures. Advanced arthritis made it impossible for him to paint his more elaborate *Abstract Heads*. "I had to find a new technique for my sick hands", he wrote. The *Meditations* are small paintings featuring the same highly simplified face, outlined in black and filled in with different combinations of colours. The title of the series reflects Jawlensky's habit of meditating before painting to achieve the proper spiritual state. As he wrote to his friend Nolde, "I paint with fervour, like a prayer."

MUNICH

Dissatisfied with his training at the Imperial Academy of Arts in St. Petersburg, he and Werefkin moved to Munich in 1896 – a real art hub of the time. Her father had died that year and left her a substantial inheritance. They settled in the artists' quarter of Schwabing, on Giselastrasse, surrounded by Russian friends, and were soon referred to as the "Giselists". Werefkin rented an entire floor with two apartments, one for Jawlensky and one for herself. During their 18 years in Bavaria, Jawlensky and Werefkin were at the heart of the development of modern art in Munich.

MÜNTER

At the beginning of the 20th century, Gabriele Münter (1877-1962) was in a relationship with Kandinsky, and the couple became friends with Jawlensky and Werefkin. Münter was a member of Der Blaue Reiter and its precursor, NKVM. Like most women artists of her time, she has long stood in the shadow of her male counterparts. In recent years, that has begun to change, as seen in the major Münter exhibition at the Louisiana in 2020. The summers that she and Kandinsky spent with Werefkin and Jawlensky in her house in Murnau were important for her: "It was a wonderful, interesting, enjoyable time, [...] I particularly enjoyed showing my work to Jawlensky [who] passed on what he had experienced and learned [and] talked about 'synthesis'."

GABRIELE MÜNTER, *JAWLENSKY AND WEREFKIN*, 1908-1909
STÄDTISCHE GALERIE IM LENBACHHAUS, MUNICH

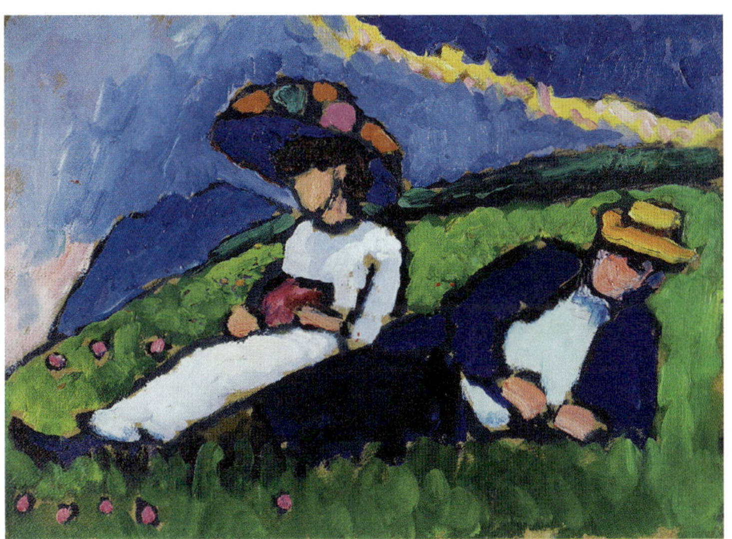

MURNAU

From 1908 to 1910, Jawlensky and Werefkin spent their summers in Münter's house in Murnau am Staffelsee with Kandinsky and Münter. There, in the foothills of the Alps, the four artists influenced each other and painted a number of very similar landscapes with the Bavarian peaks in the background, often rendered in blue. The summers in Murnau were crucial to their artistic development.

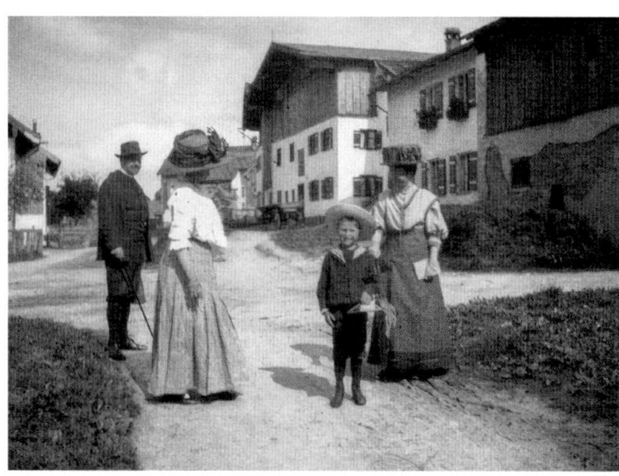

JAWLENSKY, WEREFKIN, ANDREAS JAWLENSKY, AND GABRIELE MÜNTER ON SOLLERSTRASSE IN MURNAU, AROUND 1909. PHOTO BY WASSILY KANDINSKY

MUSIC

Jawlensky's memoirs includes numerous reflections on his musical experiences. He for instance describes how he cried the first time he heard Beethoven. Jawlensky knew several leading composers of his time. In 1911, he attended a Schönberg concert in Munich, and in 1915 he visited Igor Stravinsky in the Swiss city of Morges. Music also served as a model for Jawlensky's artistic project, inspired by Kandinsky's theories of synaesthesia, which linked painting and music. The title of Jawlensky's first truly serial project, *Variations*, is derived from musical terminology. He later described these works as songs without words. In the 1930s, John Cage, a student of Schönberg, purchased three works by Jawlensky because of their musical qualities.

NKVM

In 1909, Jawlensky, with Werefkin, Münter, Kandinsky and others, founded the Neue Künstlervereinigung München (NKVM), an influential artists' association that can be seen as a precursor to Der Blaue Reiter. The move was a response to their repeated rejection by the Munich Secession. NKVM's manifesto states, "We start from the idea that the artist, in addition to the impressions he receives from the external world, is constantly gathering experiences in an inner world." The association dissolved in 1912 shortly after Franz Marc, Kandinsky and Münter left to form Der Blaue Reiter at the end of 1911.

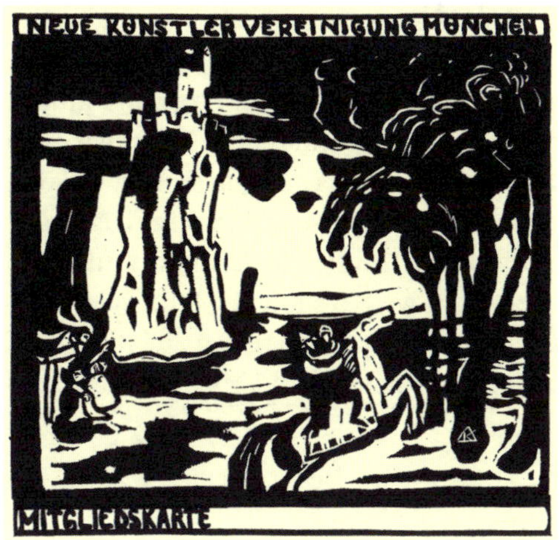

WASILY KANDINSKY, *ROCK* (MEMBERSHIP CARD FOR THE NEW ARTISTS' ASSOCIATION MUNICH), 1908-1909

NOLDE

Jawlensky first saw the work of the Expressionist painter Emil Nolde (1867-1956) in 1912 at Schmidt and Dietzel's Neue Kunstsalon in Munich. He was especially impressed by Nolde's religious pictures, in particular *Maria Aegyptiaca* and the big altarpiece *The Life of Christ*. A lifelong friendship ensued. The two artists also traded works. Jawlensky sent two of his *Meditations* to Nolde and owned several small works by Nolde as well as *Man and Woman in a Tent* (1916), a large painting that stems from Nolde's series of New Guinean subjects. Nolde's work spoke to Jawlensky's interest in reinterpreting religious imagery and reflected the contemporary fascination with 'exotic' cultures. In a 1936 letter to Nolde, Jawlensky writes, "I am happy that I own some of your works, which always speak deeply to my soul."

EMIL NOLDE, *MAN AND WOMAN IN THE TENT*, 1916
FAAH COLLECTION

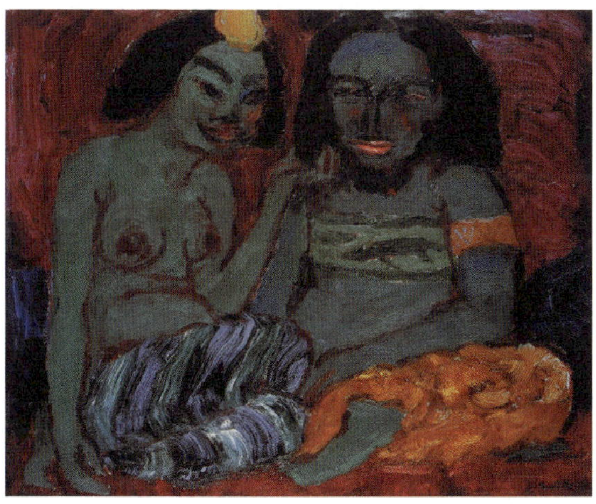

PARIS

Meeting art and artists in early-20th-century Paris had a significant impact on Jawlensky's artistic development, as it did on most artists of the time, and he came to the city many times. He first visited in 1903 and had his first exhibition there two years later at the Salon d'Automne. The following year, the Russian art critic Sergej Diaghilev organised the exhibition *L'art russe* at the Salon d'Automne and asked Jawlensky to participate. The concept was to show the latest works by Russian artists, including Natalia Gontcharova, alongside historical and more traditional paintings from the 18th and 19th centuries, as well as Russian icons.

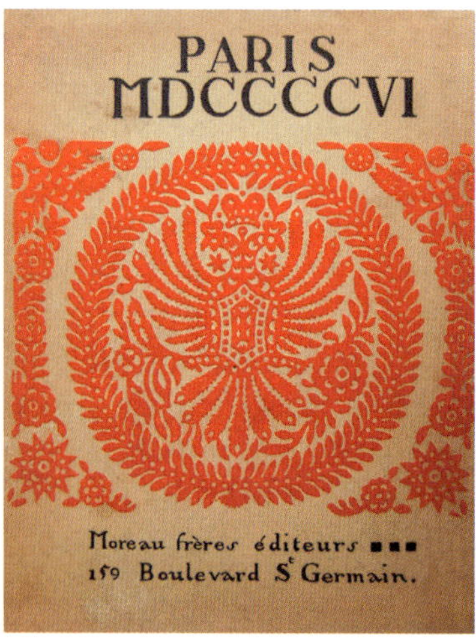

CATALOGUE FOR THE EXHIBITION *L'ART RUSSE* AT SALON D'AUTOMNE, 1906

PREROW

After three consecutive summers in Murnau with Kandinsky and Münter, Jawlensky and Werefkin spent the summer of 1911 in the Baltic seaside resort of Prerow. "For me that summer meant a great step forward in my art. I painted my finest landscapes there, as well as large figure paintings in powerful, glowing colours and not at all naturalistic and objective. I used a great deal of red, blue, orange, cadmium yellow, and chromium-oxide green. My forms were very strongly contoured in Prussian blue and came with tremendous power from an inner ecstasy."

RELIGION

Jawlensky was a man of profound faith, and his artistic ideal was religious imagery. He combined his Russian Orthodox Church upbringing with Eastern religions, which he studied in depth. Indeed, he titled his last series *Meditations*. In his memoirs he wrote, "I am Russian born. As such my heart and soul was always close to old Russian art, to Russian icons, the art of Byzantium, the mosaics of Ravenna, Venice and Rome and the art of the Romanesque period. All these arts would set up a holy vibration in my soul for they spoke to me in a language of deep spirituality. It was this art that gave me my tradition."

REPIN

At the Imperial Academy of Arts in St. Petersburg, Jawlensky befriended the famous Russian painter Ilya Repin (1844-1930). Repin painted great events in Russian history, portraits and social-realistic subjects, such as *Barge Haulers on the Volga* (1873). Unlike Jawlensky, Repin had no interest in reinventing painting. Even so, he played an important role in Jawlensky's development as an artist in the years before Jawlensky moved to Munich in 1896. However, the most pivotal event for Jawlensky during his time at Repin's painting school was meeting Marianne Werefkin.

THE ROSE-COLOURED SALON

An epicentre in the development of modern painting in the early 20th century was the home of Werefkin and Jawlensky. From 1896 to 1914, the two artists lived in apartments next to each other at Giselastrasse 23 in Munich. Dubbed the "Giselists" by their peers, they hosted a salon known as the Salon of the Giselists. The painter Vladimir Bekhteev later renamed it the Rose-Coloured Salon. While Jawlensky is far better known than Werefkin, her role in conducting art discussions at the salon should not be underestimated. The salon was visited by Kandinsky, Franz Marc, August Macke and many other well-known artists of the time.

JAWLENSKY AND WEREFKIN AT GISELASTRASSE 23, MUNICH

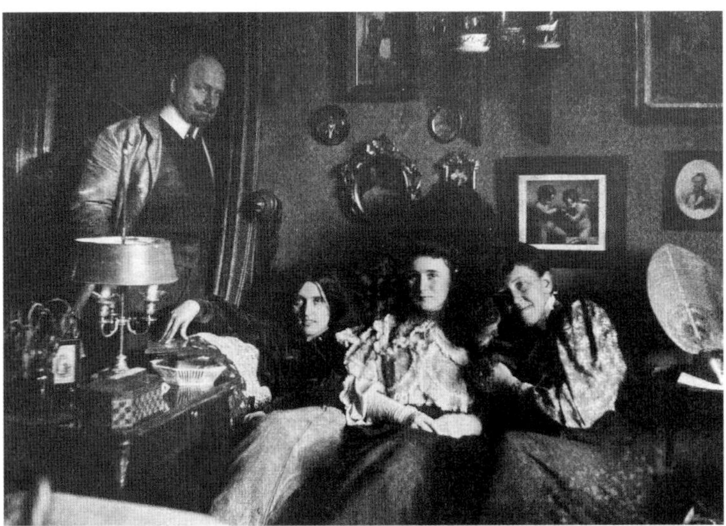

SAINT-PREX

Jawlensky and Werefkin were forced to hastily flee Munich in 1914 at the outbreak of World War I and settled in Saint-Prex, a small town on Lake Geneva. With no studio and in new surroundings, Jawlensky made a complete break with his previous painting style. This period marks the beginning of his truly original contribution to art history: serial painting. In his series *Variations*, he initially painted the view from his window over and over again.

SALON D'AUTOMNE

In 1905, Jawlensky showed in one of the most memorable editions of the annual Salon d'Automne exhibition in Paris. The exhibition is re-membered today mainly because of the Fauvists, including Matisse, André Derain, Maurice de Vlaminck, Georges Rouault and a very young Georges Braque. The Fauvists caused a scandal with their wild and non-naturalistic colours applied to quotidian subject matter, as seen for instance in the Matisse portrait *Woman with a Hat* (1905). The exhibition provided a generation of young artists with a whole new language and had a major impact on Jawlensky as well.

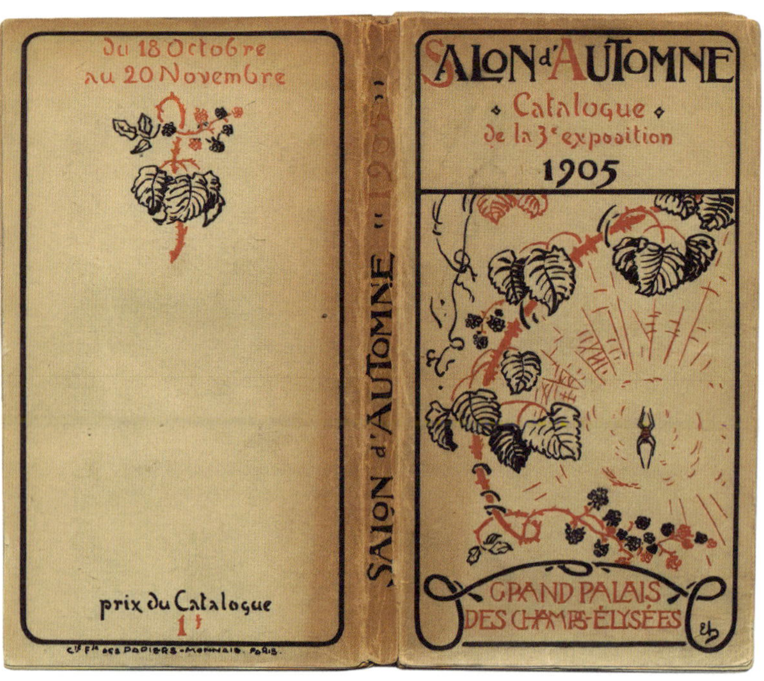

SCHEYER

In 1916, Emmy "Galka" Scheyer (1889-1945) visited Jawlensky in Saint-Prex, having been captivated by his painting *The Hunchback* (1911). Scheyer decided to give up her own artistic work to promote Jawlensky. She organised numerous exhibitions of work by Jawlensky and his group the Blue Four in Europe and the United States. As one result of her efforts, the young artist-composer John Cage discovered Jawlensky and bought a painting by him.

SERIALITY

The beginning of Jawlensky's serial works is generally dated to 1914, though he had in fact worked on serial projects before – only using a different process. In 1912, he painted a portrait series of women of different nationalities, with titles like *Byzantine Woman*, *Egyptian Woman* and *French Woman*. However, Jawlensky did not engage in seriality in the sense of 'repeating the same subject' until he began his *Variations* in Saint-Prex in 1914. This was a brand-new device with very few precedents. Over and over again, he painted the same motif – initially, the view from his window, then faces/heads which became his *Meditations* – like a man possessed, until he was no longer able to paint.

STEINER / THEOSOPHY

From 1905-1910, Rudolf Steiner (1861-1925) gave a series of lectures in Munich that influenced the city's avant-garde artists, not least those who frequented the Rose-Coloured Salon. According to Werefkin, in 1908 Jawlensky had an opportunity to discuss painting with Steiner, who in his lectures had proposed merging the Eastern and Western religious experiences. Steiner had a major impact on Kandinsky and most likely on Jawlensky as well. Jawlensky read about Buddhism and Hinduism and practiced yoga, though he never lost his connection to his Russian Orthodox faith. He both prayed and meditated. His works and titles often reference Eastern and Western religions.

TRETYAKOV

Jawlensky's early encounters with art were at the big art museums in Moscow, where he practiced drawing. "I used to go to the Tretyakov Gallery every Sunday, arriving very early and staying there without eating until closing time at three o'clock. It was a tremendous experience for me, like going to church. Indeed, I felt as if I was in a temple. After that, I used what little free time I had to visit all the art exhibitions; I was like a man obsessed. I did not know any painters, though; I had no time because I had a great deal to learn. Not being much of a scholar I had to work very hard."

VAN GOGH

Like Gauguin and Cézanne, Vincent van Gogh (1853-1890) was a major influence on a new generation of artists in the early part of the 20th century. In 1908, Jawlensky and Werefkin bought Van Gogh's *The House of Père Pilon* (1890) from an art dealer in Munich. Jawlensky and Werefkin owned the painting until 1925, when they had to sell it for financial reasons.

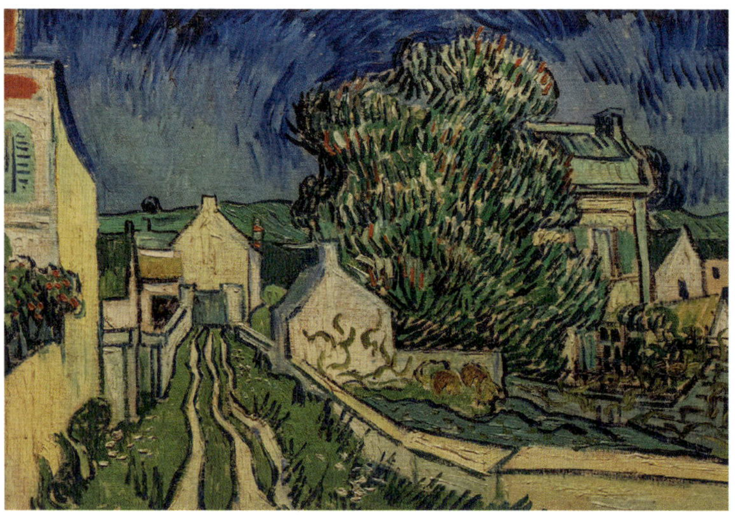

VARIATIONS

At this remove, it can be difficult to appreciate how radical Jawlensky's *Variations* were in 1914. At the outbreak of World War I, Jawlensky and Werefkin fled to Saint-Prex. Because he had no studio, Jawlensky resorted to repeatedly painting the view from his window. Over time, the depiction of the view, what he actually saw, became secondary. Jawlensky kept on painting his *Variations* until 1921, even after moving to Zurich and, later, Ascona. The serial approach of the *Variations* subverts the traditional notion of the 'masterpiece' as a singular work. Instead, Jawlensky developed an artistic project in which the meaning emerges when comparing the individual paintings.

WAR

The outbreak of World War I in 1914 upended Jawlensky and Werefkin's lives. Like all Russians, who were now enemies of Germany, they were given 48 hours to leave the country. They hastily fled to Switzerland, leaving behind many of their belongings. Werefkin never returned to Germany, while Jawlensky moved to Wiesbaden in 1921 and stayed there until his death. By the 1930s, with war again looming over Europe, Jawlensky had become a German citizen. All the same, the Nazis considered his art dangerous, branding it "degenerate".

WEREFKIN

Marianne Werefkin (1860-1938) takes up remarkably little space in Jawlensky's late memoirs. However, he does write, "Meeting her changed my life, and this intelligent, very talented woman and I became close friends." They met through the painter Ilya Repin in 1892 and moved to Munich together in 1896. Theirs was hardly a conventional relationship. Jawlensky was financially dependent on Werefkin, and they stayed together in one form or another until 1921. When they moved to Munich in 1896, Werefkin had stopped painting and devoted herself to supporting Jawlensky. About this decision, she later wrote, "Why not go on working? I had lost confidence. The habit of putting myself in second place decided it. Am I a true artist? Yes, yes, yes. Am I a woman? Yes, yes, yes. Can the two march side by side? No, no, no." Nonetheless, Werefkin is a central figure in art history, not least for creating a setting in Munich for discussing avant-garde art.

JAWLENSKY'S LONG-TIME COMPANION AND COLLABORATOR, MARIANNE WEREFKIN

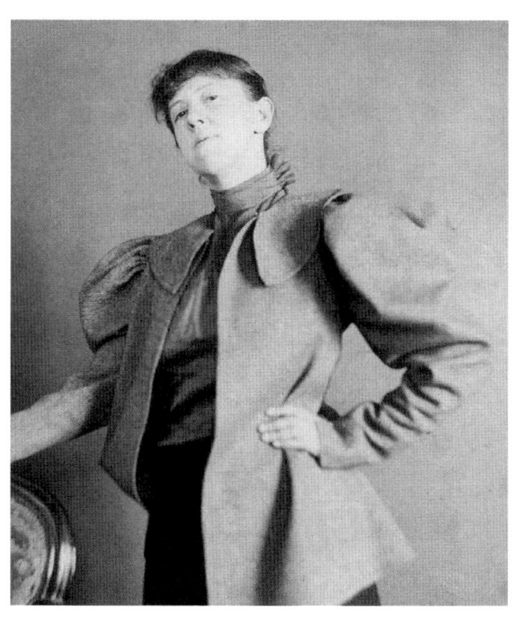

WIESBADEN

In 1921, Jawlensky moved to Wiesbaden with his son, Andreas, and Helene Nesnakomoff, motivated by his success with a previous exhibition there. He lived in the city until his death in 1941. Today, Museum Wiesbaden holds one of the biggest collections of Jawlensky's works in the world.

WOMEN

The old saying that "Behind every successful man stands a woman" is also true for Jawlensky. In his case, there were three. The first was Werefkin, who gave up painting to support Jawlensky, financing his career with an inheritance from her father. Then there was Helene Nesnakomoff, who gave birth to his son and accepted a subordinate role in their unusual and, for a long time, unresolved relationship. Finally, there was Emmy "Galka" Scheyer, a young artist who abandoned her own career after seeing Jawlensky's *The Hunchback* (1911) and devoted herself to promoting him.

JAWLENSKY IN LOCARNO, SWITZERLAND, 1919-1920,
WITH HELENE NESNAKOMOFF, ALEXANDER SACHAROFF,
EMMY "GALKA" SCHEYER, CLOTILDE VON DERP
AND MARIANNE WEREFKIN

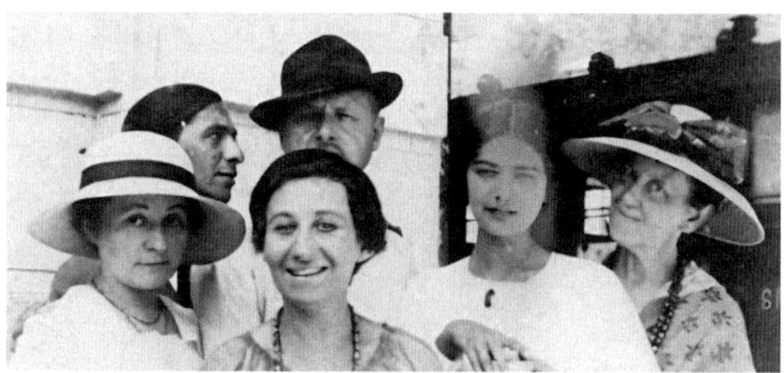

WRITING

Jawlensky was no theorist and left no body of writing on art. Even so, we have a large number of words by him. Both his memoirs and the many letters he exchanged with fellow artists offer insight into his perception of art, particularly painting. Jawlensky's late works often feature poetic titles, such as *In Love, the Spiritual is Eternal* in this exhibition.

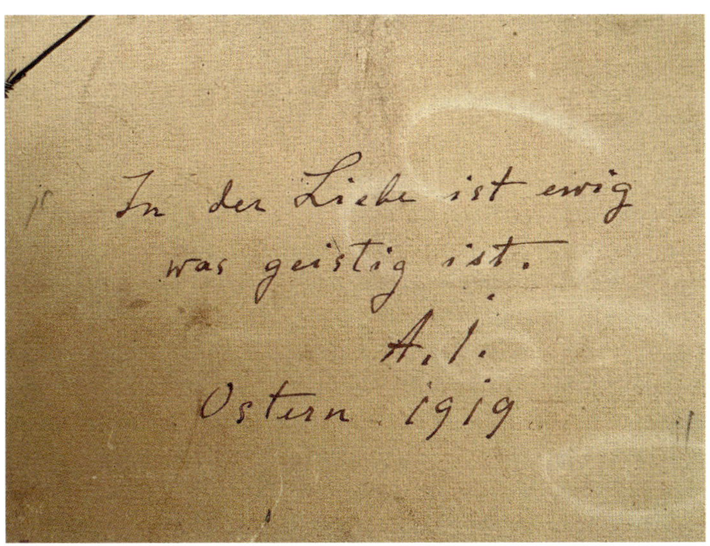

ZURICH

In the spring of 1917, Jawlensky and his family relocated from Saint-Prex to Zurich. There, they met several members of the Dada group, including Tristan Tzara, Hans Arp, Sophie Taeuber-Arp and Hugo Ball. Zurich marks the beginning of Jawlensky's final project, which has several stages. It was there that he began painting his series of faces/heads. The first of these, *Mystical Heads*, is stylised portraits of women he knew.

Comprised by Mathias Ussing Seeberg

Encyclopedia Jawlensky has been comprised with the help of a long list of publications about the artist including: Clemens Weiler, *Alexej Jawlensky*, Köln: Verlag M. DuMont Schauberg, 1959 / Clemens Weiler, *Jawlensky: Heads, Faces, Meditations*, Karlsruhe: Pall Mall Press, 1971 / Vivian Endicott Barnett (ed.), *Alexei Jawlensky*, Prestel Verlag, Wemding, 2017 / Roman Zieglgänsberger, Annegret Hoberg and Matthias Mühling (eds.), *Soulmates, Alexej von Jawlensky and Marianne von Werefkin*, Italy: Prestel Verlag, 2020 / Roman Zieglgänsberger (ed.), *Alles! 100 Jahre Jawlensky in Wiesbaden*, Hirmer Verlag, Altusried, 2021 / Itzhak Goldberg, *Jawlensky – The Promised Face*, France: L'Harmattan, 2020 / As well as the website www.jawlensky.ch which is part of and updated by Die Alexej von Jawlensky-Archiv S.A., which was founded by Angelica Jawlensky Bianconi, Maria Jawlensky and Lucia Pieroni-Jawlensky in 1988.

A LETTER TO FATHER WILLIBRORD VERKADE

FROM ALEXEJ JAWLENSKY

To Father Willibrord Verkade   Wiesbaden, 12 June 1938
My dear Father,

I should have written and indeed wanted to write to you ages ago
but my long illness prevented me. At the time I received your book
Der Antrieb ins Vollkommene I was in bed with much pain. Your book
brought back beautiful memories. You have always been in my heart.
Please forgive me for not having thanked you for the book before,
and please now accept my most heartfelt gratitude.

I cannot write to you myself but have to dictate my letters, and
I am sorry because since we were last together so much has changed
in the whole world and also in me. And on top of that, for the last
nine years I have been very ill and in much pain and have become a
cripple. My hands have grown quite stiff and I have to lie down
almost all the time. But because I have always lived deeply in art no
matter what has befallen me, I should like to tell you about my
artistic development, which is also my spiritual development.

In 1911 I found a personal form and palette and painted powerful
figure paintings and heads with which I made a name for myself.
I went on working like that until 1914.

Just before the war I suffered a great deal emotionally on account
of family matters, and then came the war and we had to flee with
nothing but what we could carry. We went to Switzerland, to a little
place called Saint-Prex, near Morges on the Lake of Geneva. In our
small flat there I had only one little room in which to work, with a
single window. I tried to go on with my powerful, strongly coloured
paintings but I found I couldn't. My soul would not allow that
sensuous painting, although there was much beauty in my works.

I felt I had to find another language, a more spiritual language.
I felt it in my soul. I sat at my window. Before me I saw a path, a few
trees, and from time to time a mountain was visible in the distance.

I now began to search for a new way in art. It was an enormous
task. I realized that I must paint not what I saw, not even what I felt,
but simply the thing that lived within me, in my soul. Metaphorically
speaking it was like this: I felt inside me, in my chest, an organ, and
I had to make that organ sound. And the nature I had before me was
only my prompter. It was a key with which I could unlock the organ
and make it sound. At the beginning it was very difficult. But little
by little it became easier for me to find in terms of colours

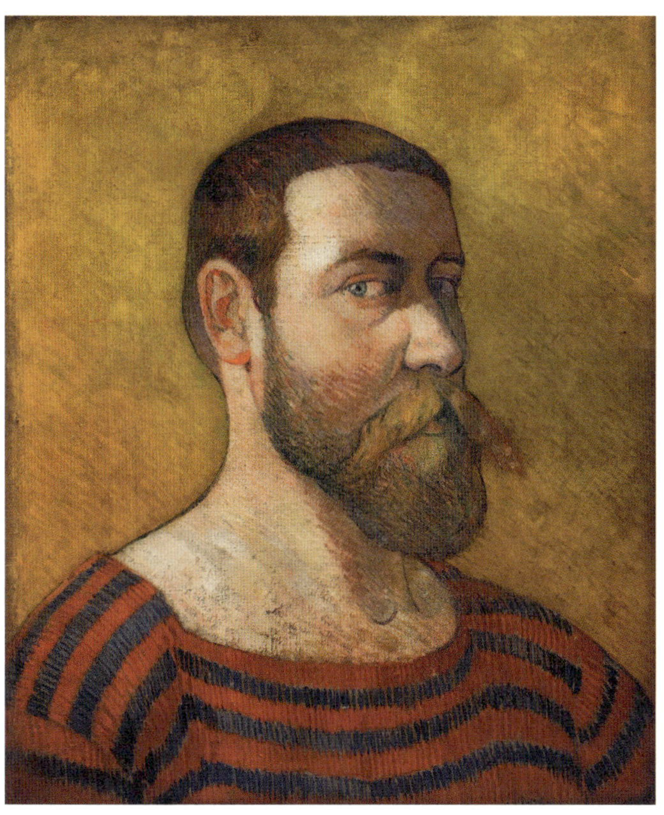

and forms the thing that lay in my soul. My format became small: 30 × 40. I painted a great many pictures, which I called "Variations on a Landscape Theme".

They are songs without words. I went on painting these variations for several years, and then it became necessary for me to find a form for the face, for I realized that great art was only to be painted with religious feeling. And that was something I could bring only to the human face. I realized that the artist must express in his art through forms and colours that within him which is divine. That is why the work of art is a visible God, and why art is "a longing for God". For many years I did not need the prompting of nature. It was enough for me to become absorbed within myself, to pray, and to compose my soul in an attitude of religious devotion. I painted many, many "Faces". They too are only 32 × 42. They are very perfect technically and radiate great spirituality.

So the years passed in much work. And then I became ill, but I was able to go on working although my hands grew stiffer and stiffer. I could no longer hold the brush with one hand but had to use both, in great pain the whole time. My format became very small and I also had to find a new technique. For three years I painted these small abstract heads like a man obsessed. Because I felt I would soon have to stop working for good. And that indeed is what happened!

I am sending you one of my last works. I suppose it will be strange to you. But, dear Father, don't straight away judge it harshly, for you surely know that every language when it is new can seem strange and even repellent. One must make the effort to understand, as with any new language that one has to learn from scratch. One mustn't let one's soul protest – the soul has to exert itself and to suffer. And in that way one comes to understand. It's always like that.

I'm also sending you a coloured reproduction of a "Variation". The original belongs to Professor Hamann, Marburg an der Lahn, who had it reproduced in the art books of Marburg University.

I am a cripple now. I cannot work, I can neither walk nor stand but must lie down the whole time, and I suffer terribly. I embrace you heart and soul and ask you for your blessing.

I love you dearly,
Your Alexej Jawlensky

Published in Clemens Weiler, Jawlensky: *Heads, Faces, Meditations*, Pall Mall Press, Karlsruhe, 1971, translated by Edith Küstner & J.A. Underwood.

Jan (Willibrord) Verkade (1868-1946) was a Dutch Post-Impressionist and Christian Symbolist painter. A disciple of Paul Gauguin, he was associated with the French artist group Les Nabis. He converted to Catholicism in 1892 and, under the name Willibrord Verkade, became a monk at the Benedictine monastery in Beuron, Southern Germany. In 1907, Jawlensky met Verkade, from whom he learned about Gauguin's ideas, and the two artists became close friends. During his stay in Munich, Verkade often painted in Jawlensky's studio. In 1907 or 1908, Verkade painted a nude on the reverse of Jawlensky's *Still Life with Oranges*, and the two artists then gave the double-sided painting as a gift to their mutual friend the artist Karl Caspar. It remained in his collection for several decades before the two works were separated in the 1950s.

ALEXEJ JAWLENSKY
STILL LIFE WITH ORANGES, C. 1902
OIL ON CARDBOARD, LAID ON PANEL, 31 × 37.5 CM
PRIVATE COLLECTION

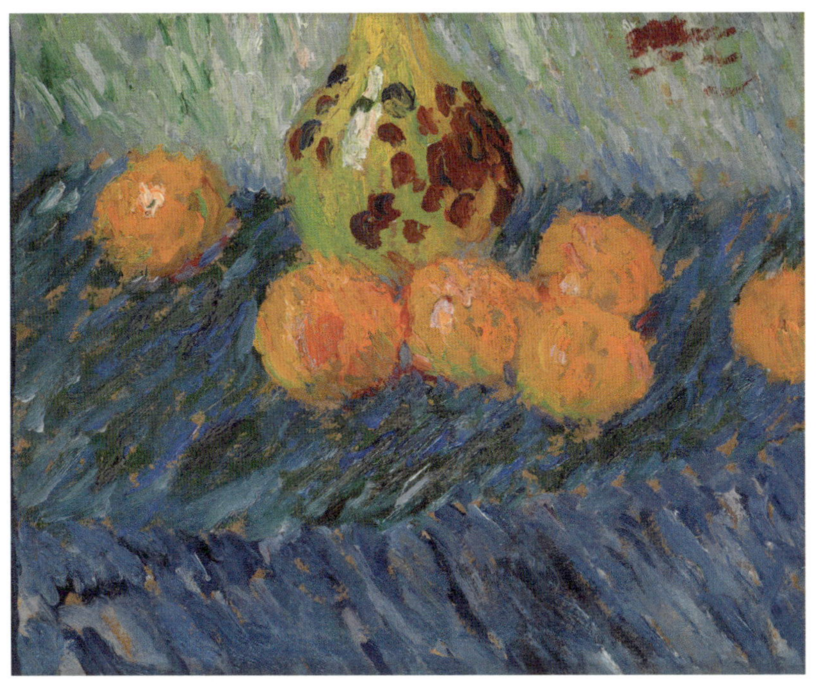

LIST OF WORKS

16 Dorf Murnau, 1908
Murnau Village
Oil on cardboard, 49 × 53.5 cm
Kunstmuseum Basel, Stiftung Im
Obersteg, Deposit Kunstmuseum
Basel 2004

11 Stillleben mit schwarzer Vase, 1909
Still Life with Black Vase
Oil on cardboard, 52,6 × 32,8 cm
Museum Wiesbaden

12 Murnauer Landschaft, 1909
Murnau Landscape
Oil on cardboard, 50.5 × 54.5 cm
Städtische Galerie im Lenbachhaus
und Kunstbau München, Gabriele
Münter Stiftung 1957

33 Kind, c. 1909
Child
Oil and tempera on linen textured
cardboard, 53.5 × 50 cm
Kunstmuseum Basel, Stiftung Im
Obersteg, Deposit Kunstmuseum
Basel 2004

15 Selbstbildnis, 1911
Self-Portrait
Oil on linen textured cardboard
54 × 51 cm
Kunstmuseum Basel, Stiftung Im
Obersteg, Deposit Kunstmuseum
Basel 2004

14 An der Ostsee, 1911
By the Baltic Sea
Oil on linen textured cardboard
50 × 54 cm
Kunstmuseum Basel, Stiftung Im
Obersteg, Deposit Kunstmuseum
Basel 2004

27 Jünglingskopf, 1911
Head of a Youth
Oil on cardboard, 53.5 × 49.5 cm
Kunstmuseum Basel, Stiftung Im
Obersteg, Deposit Kunstmuseum
Basel 2004

10 Stillleben mit grüner Vase, c. 1911
Still Life with Green Vase
Oil on cardboard on canvas
49.5 × 53.5 cm
Museum Wiesbaden

9 Konstantinowka mit
geneigtem Kopf, c. 1912
Konstantinowka with Head Tilted
Indian ink on handmade paper
46.5 × 38 cm
Museum Wiesbaden

30 Liegender weiblicher Akt, mit den
Armen über dem Kopf, c. 1912
Reclining Female Nude with Arms
Above Head
Chalk on parchment on Japan paper
48.8 × 61.9 cm
Museum Wiesbaden

28 Liegende, c. 1912
Reclining
Charcoal on paper, 47.2 × 62 cm
Museum Wiesbaden

31 Sitzender weiblicher Akt, 1913
Sitting Female Nude
Chalk on parchment paper
49.1 × 30.7 cm
Museum Wiesbaden

29 Liegender weiblicher Akt, 1913
Reclining Female Nude
Charcoal on parchment paper
30.5 × 49 cm
Museum Wiesbaden

25 Braune Locken, 1913
Brown Locks
Oil on cardboard, 53,5 × 49.5 cm
Kunstmuseum Basel, Stiftung Im
Obersteg, Deposit Kunstmuseum
Basel 2004

30 Liegender weiblicher Akt, c. 1913
Reclining Female Nude
Charcoal on handmade paper
32 × 43.5 cm
Museum Wiesbaden

52 Gewitterlandschaft, 1915
Thunderstorm Landscape
Oil on linen textured cardboard
27 × 36 cm
Kunstmuseum Basel, Stiftung Im
Obersteg, Deposit Kunstmuseum
Basel 2004

37 Grosse Variation, 1915
Large Variation
Oil and pencil on linen textured
paper on hardboard, 52 × 37.5 cm
Kunstmuseum Basel, Stiftung Im
Obersteg, Deposit Kunstmuseum
Basel 2004

39 Variation: Nacht, 1916
Variation: Night
Oil on linen textured paper on
cardboard, 35.5 × 27 cm
Kunstmuseum Basel, Purchase 1941

35 Variation: Der orange Weg, 1916
Variation: The Orange Road
Oil and charcoal on linen textured
cardboard, 37.5 × 26 cm
Kunstmuseum Basel, Stiftung Im
Obersteg, Deposit Kunstmuseum
Basel 2004

51 Variation: Kühler Frühling, 1916
Variation: Cold Spring
Oil on paper on cardboard
36.1 × 27 cm
Private collection

38 Variation: Dämmerung, c. 1916
Variation: Twilight
Oil on linen textured cardboard
36 × 27 cm
Kunstmuseum Basel, Stiftung Im
Obersteg, Deposit Kunstmuseum
Basel 2004

55 Exotischer Kopf, 1917
Exotic Head
Oil on paper, 53.5 × 38.5 cm
Museum Wiesbaden

57 Mystischer Kopf: Mädchenkopf
(frontal), 1918
Mystic Head: Girl's Head (front)
Oil and pencil on paper on cardboard
40 × 30 cm
Kunstmuseum Basel, Stiftung Im
Obersteg, Deposit Kunstmuseum
Basel 2004

59 Mystischer Kopf: Mädchenkopf
(Halbseitlich), 1918
Mystic Head: Girl's Head (slightly
turned)
Oil and pencil on paper on cardboard
40 × 30 cm
Kunstmuseum Basel, Stiftung Im
Obersteg, Deposit Kunstmuseum
Basel 2004

40 Variation: Purpurgold (Herbst), c. 1918
Variation: Purple-Gold (Autumn)
Oil on linen textured paper on
cardboard, 36.3 × 25.5 cm
Private collection

49 Variation, c. 1918
Oil on linen textured paper on
cardboard, 36.2 × 28.2 cm
Private collection

63 Heilandsgesicht: In der Liebe ist
ewig was geistig ist, 1919
Saviour's Face: In Love, the
Spiritual is Eternal
Oil on linen textured paper on
cardboard, 30.5 × 22 cm
Private Collection, Riehen,
Switzerland

61 Heilandsgesicht: Wächter, 1920
Saviour's Face: Guardian
Oil on cardboard, 37.5 × 26.5 cm
Kunsthalle Mannheim

62 Heilandsgesicht: Dornen, 1920
Saviour's Face: Thorns
Oil on linen textured paper on
cardboard, 35.6 × 26.7 cm
Private Collection, Riehen,
Switzerland

65 Abstrakter Kopf: Schwarz-Gelb-
Violett, c. 1922
Abstract Head: Black-Yellow-Purple
Oil on linen textured cardboard
36 × 27.5 cm
Kunstmuseum Basel, Stiftung Im
Obersteg, Deposit Kunstmuseum
Basel 2004

73 Abstrakter Kopf: Mysterium, 1925
Abstract Head: Mystery
Oil on linen textured cardboard
42.5 × 32.5 cm
Kunstmuseum Basel, Stiftung Im
Obersteg, Deposit Kunstmuseum
Basel 2004

71 Abstrakter Kopf: Inneres Schauen
Grün-Gold, 1926
Abstract Head: An Inner Gaze,
Golden Green
Oil on linen textured cardboard
34.5 × 24.5 cm
Kunstmuseum Basel, Stiftung Im
Obersteg, Deposit Kunstmuseum
Basel 2004

77 Abstrakter Kopf: Abend, 1927
Abstract Head: Evening
Oil and charcoal on linen textured
cardboard, 43 × 33.5 cm
Kunstmuseum Basel, Stiftung Im
Obersteg, Deposit Kunstmuseum
Basel 2004

67 Abstrakter Kopf: Winter, 1927
Abstract Head: Winter
Oil on cardboard on wood
42.2 × 32.8 cm
Galerie Ludorff, Düsseldorf

75 Abstrakter Kopf: Lebenstropfen,
1928
Abstract Head: Drops of Life
Oil on linen textured paper on
cardboard, 42.8 × 33 cm
Museum Wiesbaden

66 Abstrakter Kopf: Rosa-Hellblau,
1929
Abstract Head: Pink-Light Blue
Oil on cardboard, 37 × 27 cm
Kunstmuseum Basel, Stiftung Im
Obersteg, Deposit Kunstmuseum
Basel 2004

69 Abstrakter Kopf (Konstruktiver
Kopf), c. 1930
Abstract Head (Constructivist Head)
Oil on paper on cardboard
42. 5 × 32.5 cm
Kunstmuseum Basel, Bequest Dr.
August Meyer, Basel 1977

76 Abstrakter Kopf: Gold und Rosa, 1931
Abstract Head: Gold and Pink
Oil on linen textured cardboard
42.5 × 32.5 cm
Kunstmuseum Basel, Stiftung Im
Obersteg, Deposit Kunstmuseum
Basel 2004

74 Abstrakter Kopf: Apoll, 1931
Abstract Head: Apollo
Oil on linen textured cardboard on
blockboard, 43 × 33 cm
Kunstmuseum Basel, Stiftung Im
Obersteg, Deposit Kunstmuseum
Basel 2004

79 Kopf (Abstrakter Kopf /
Meditation), 1933
Head (Abstract Head / Meditation)
Oil on linen textured paper on
cardboard, 16.8 × 15.2 cm
Museum Wiesbaden

91 Meditation: Erinnerung an meine
kranken Hände (N. 5), 1934
Meditation: In Memory of My
Ailing Hands (N. 5)
Oil on linen textured paper on
cardboard, 20 × 16 cm
Museum Wiesbaden

89 Meditation (N. 30), 1934
Oil on paper on cardboard, 15,5 × 12 cm
Kunstmuseum Basel, Stiftung Im
Obersteg, Deposit Kunstmuseum
Basel 2004

93 Meditation (N. 290), 1934
Oil on Linen textured paper on
cardboard, 17.6 × 12.6 cm
Private collection

103 Meditation: Rückblick (II N. 83), 1935
Meditation: Looking Back (II N. 83)
Oil on paper on cardboard on wood
18 × 13.5 cm
Museum Wiesbaden

101 Meditation (N. 33), 1935
Oil on paper on cardboard
20.5 × 13.5 cm
Kunstmuseum Basel, Stiftung Im
Obersteg, Deposit Kunstmuseum
Basel 2004

94 Meditation (N. 57), 1935
Oil on linen textured paper on
cardboard, 17 × 12.5 cm
Kunstmuseum Basel, Stiftung Im
Obersteg, Deposit Kunstmuseum
Basel 2004

107 Meditation (N. 133), 1935
Oil on linen textured paper on
cardboard, 18 × 13.5 cm
Kunstmuseum Basel, Stiftung Im
Obersteg, Deposit Kunstmuseum
Basel 2004

95 Meditation: Harmonie in Rot
und Blau, 1935
Meditation: Harmony in Red and Blue
Oil on cardboard, 17 × 12 cm
Private collection, Riehen,
Switzerland

99 Meditation (N. 95), 1935
Oil on linen textured paper on
cardboard, 17.7 × 13.5 cm
Private collection, Riehen,
Switzerland

98 Meditation: Kleiner Kopf (N. 120),
1935
Meditation: Small Head (N. 120)
Oil on linen textured paper on
cardboard, 17.8 × 13.6 cm
Private collection, Riehen,
Switzerland

115 Meditation: Ein Brausen kam
einher, 1935
Meditation: A Rushing Sound
Approached
Oil on paper on cardboard
19 × 12.4 cm
Galerie von Vertes, Zürich

117 Meditation: Vergesse mich
nicht, 1935
Meditation: Forget Me Not
Oil on cardboard, 19 × 12.2 cm
Private collection, Germany

109 Meditation: In mir leuchtet es,
komm zu mir, 1935
Meditation: It Shines Within Me,
Come To Me
Oil on linen textured paper on
cardboard, 17.7 × 13.6 cm
Private collection

97 Meditation (N. 87), 1935
Oil on linen textured paper on
cardboard, 17 × 12 cm
Private Collection, Riehen,
Switzerland

105 Stillleben: Gelbe Vase (III N. 32), 1936
Still Life (Yellow Vase (III N. 32)
Oil on linen textured paper on
cardboard, 18.2 × 12.5 cm
Museum Wiesbaden

111 Grosse Meditation: Glut
(VI N. 24), 1936
Large meditation: Glow (VI N. 24)
Oil on canvas on cardboard
24 × 19.5 cm
Museum Wiesbaden

113 Grosse Meditation: Trauer muss
Elektra tragen, 1936
Large Meditation: Mourning
Becomes Electra
Oil on paper on cardboard, 24 × 18 cm
Museum Wiesbaden

80 Meditation auf Goldgrund, 1936
Meditation on Golden Background
Oil on paper, 14 × 11 cm
Städtische Galerie im Lenbachhaus
und Kunstbau München, Bernhard
und Elly Koehler Stiftung 1965

108 Grosse Meditation: Im Dickicht
(N. 24), 1937
Large Meditation: In the Thicket
(N. 24)
Oil on linen textured paper on
cardboard, 24.8 × 19.3 cm
Private Collection, Riehen,
Switzerland

119 Grosse Meditation (N. 6), 1937
Large Meditation (N. 6)
Oil on linen textured paper on
cardboard, 24.8 × 19.3 cm
Private Collection, Riehen,
Switzerland

120 Grosses Stilleben: Stilleben auf
schwarzem Hintergrund, helles Glas
mit rosa und roten Rosen, 1937
Large Still Life: Still Life on Black
Background, Clear Glass with Pink
and Red Roses
Oil on board, 43,5 × 26.7 cm
Private collection

ALEXEJ JAWLENSKY
VARIATIONS

© 2025 LOUISIANA MUSEUM OF MODERN ART & THE CONTRIBUTORS

EDITED BY LÆRKE RYDAL JØRGENSEN, KASPAR THORMOD,
IBEN ENGELHARDT ANDERSEN AND MATHIAS USSING SEEBERG
GRAPHIC DESIGN: MICHAEL JENSEN
TRANSLATIONS: GLEN GARNER (MATHIAS USSING SEEBERG
AND ALEXANDER TOVBORG), ADAM KING (FOREWORD)
PROOFREADING: HENRY BROOME
PHOTO EDITORS: GRETHE RØNDAL CHRISTENSEN AND KIM HANSEN
COVER: *SAVIOUR'S FACE: IN LOVE, THE SPIRITUAL IS ETERNAL*, 1919 (DETAIL)
LITHO/PRINT: NARAYANA PRESS
ISBN: 978-87-93659-88-9
PRINTED IN DENMARK 2025
WWW.LOUISIANA.DK

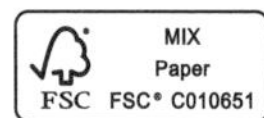

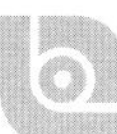

The emission of greenhouse gases
from production of this book is
0,4 kg CO2eq evaluated according
to www.climatecalc.eu.
Cert.nr. CC-000159/DK
www.narayana.dk

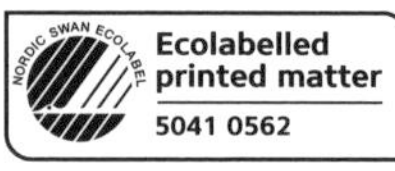

ALL WORKS BY STEFANA MCCLURE: © STEFANA MCCLURE STUDIO, COURTESY: BARTHA_CONTEMPORARY,
LONDON; GABRIELE MÜNTER: © GABRIELE MÜNTER/VISDA 2024; EMIL NOLDE: © NOLDE STIFTUNG SEEBÜLL;
ALEXANDER TOVBORG: © COURTESY BLUM GALLERY AND THE ARTIST

PHOTO: P. 9, 10, 11, 28, 29, 30, 31, 55, 75, 79, 91, 103, 105, 111, 113: MUSEUM WIESBADEN/BERND FICKERT;
12-13, 80: COURTESY STÄDTISCHE GALERIE IM LENBACHHAUS UND KUNSTBAU MÜNCHEN; 14, 15, 16, 25, 27,
33, 35, 37, 38, 39, 52-53, 57, 59, 65, 66, 69, 71, 73, 74, 76, 77, 89, 94, 101, 107, 122: KUNSTMUSEUM BASEL,
MARTIN P. BÜHLER; 19: COURTESY SOTHEBY'S 2025; 40, 117, 120: FUIS FOTOGRAFIE, COLOGNE; 42:
SHUTTERSTOCK; 45 LEFT, 45 MIDDLE: FINE ART IMAGES / BRIDGEMAN IMAGES; 45 RIGHT: CHRISTIE'S IMAGES
/ BRIDGEMAN IMAGES; 46, 47: COURTESY BARTHA_CONTEMPORARY, LONDON; 49, 93, 109: COURTESY
GRISEBACH GMBH; 51: COURTESY KETTERER KUNST GMBH UND CO; 61: KUNSTHALLE MANNHEIM / CEM
YÜCETAS; COVER, 62, 63, 95, 97, 98, 99, 108, 119: MAX EHRENGRUBER; 67: ACHIM KUKULIES, DÜSSELDORF;
82: HISTORIC IMAGES / ALAMY STOCK PHOTO; 115: WALTER BAYER, MUNICH; 121, 129, 130, 131, 137, 142:
ALEXEJ VON JAWLENSKY-ARCHIV S.A, MURALTO / SWITZERLAND; 124: FINE ART IMAGES/HERITAGE IMAGES//
ALAMY STOCK PHOTO; 125: WIKIPEDIA/SAN FRANCISCO EXAMINER, 1925; 126: SCHERL/SÜDDEUTSCHE
ZEITUNG PHOTO; 128: JOSEF ZIMMERMANN; 132: FRANK NOWIKOWSKI / ALAMY STOCK PHOTO; 133: ALBUM/
RITZAU SCANPIX; 134: COURTESY GABRIELE MÜNTER- UND JOHANNES EICHNER-STIFTUNG, MÜNCHEN; 135
THE BOTTOM: COURTESY FAAH COLLECTION; 136 GETTY RESEARCH INSTITUTE; 140: FRANCK LEGROS /
ALAMY STOCK PHOTO; 143: HEINRICH VISCHER

THE CATALOGUE IS PUBLISHED ON THE OCCASION OF THE EXHIBITION
ALEXEJ JAWLENSKY
VARIATIONS
THE EXHIBITION IS PART OF THE SERIES *LOUISIANA ON PAPER*

LOUISIANA MUSEUM OF MODERN ART, HUMLEBÆK
30 JANUARY – 1 JUNE 2025

CURATOR: MATHIAS USSING SEEBERG
CURATORIAL COORDINATOR/REGISTRAR: EVA LUND
CONSERVATOR/EXHIBITION PRODUCER: JESPER LUND MADSEN
GRAPHIC DESIGN: MARIE D'ORIGNY LÜBECKER,
MARIA HVIID BENGTSON AND THOMAS JOAKIM WINTHER

THE EXHIBITION AT THE LOUISIANA MUSEUM
OF MODERN ART IS SUPPORTED BY:

 C.L. DAVIDS FOND OG SAMLING

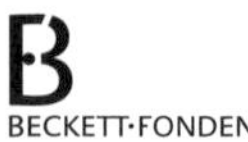
BECKETT·FONDEN